DIVERSITY AT WORK

DIVERSITY AT WORK

What Every Leader Should

Know to be More Effective

Dr. Paul L. Gerhardt
"The Organizational Doctor"

To order additional copies of this book, contact:
Xlibris Corporation
1-888-795-4274
www.Xlibris.com
Orders@Xlibris.com

36046

CONTENTS

To my mother and father who first taught me the value of diversity.
Also, to my loving wife Cindy and daughter Nickole.

PREFACE

Aside from eating right, exercising regularly, getting enough sleep, and spiritual replenishment, continual learning for personal growth is the healthiest thing we can do for ourselves. In the spirit of personal learning and growth, this book is one of a series of books dedicated to helping individuals become better leaders and more successful contributors to their organizations, communities, and families. The information found in this book compiles several years of research and personal observations from interactions with others in my practice as an organizational development consultant, teacher and lecturer.

Hopefully, you will intellectually benefit from the teachings of this book and take time daily to ponder different aspects of the contents. I hope you will agree that books such as this one can be life changing when they provide something we are lacking. However, what I share with my readers in this text are only recommendations. My personal wish is to help people stretch thinking and interpersonal abilities to new levels of understanding, so they might find more personal and professional satisfaction in life. I believe that people cannot find internal happiness and peace unless they constantly live their lives in a quest to be the very best they can be, as opposed to living in fear of the unknown.

In a similar vein, organizations cannot be successful unless they promote continued growth and education for their members. Hopefully, this book will serve as a practical tool for both organizational and individual edification and will make a difference if readers apply its contents to the organizations they serve.

For example, diversity programs are a crucial element of creating and maintaining successful organizations. Diversity includes both cultural and other backgrounds (discussed in this book).

Understanding diversity can be not only interesting, but life-changing. It is a journey that needs to be taken on an individual basis and an exploration into one's own values and beliefs. The journey can be a very enjoyable one and one that may even set you free when it touches the soul in a real way.

This can only occur if all managers and people in leadership positions truly understand how diversity benefits the organization itself. Ideally, every individual in the organization should be involved to make this work. This can only occur in a holistic way, meaning that it starts at a very personal level and must somehow become a part of every individual within the organization. Systems will need to be developed to monitor and maintain the highest levels of support for an undertaking such as a diversity program.

Employers who properly implement diversity programs also reap many benefits from them. A well-managed organization implements diversity programs for many reasons, such as:

- After implementing a diversity program, employees and customers feel more welcome where they work and do business. As a result, they will continue to be associated with the organization and generally find ways to support it, helping it to prosper.

- Employees must learn how to work more effectively with people of all backgrounds and need tools to develop individual multicultural abilities and understandings.
- Learning how to work with others means finding how to best communicate with them, as I discuss further in this book.
- Finally, well-managed organizations must establish multicultural management teams or diversity task forces. I expound on these concepts in later chapters.

Understanding how to manage diversity is a fundamental leadership skill. Once a diversity program is established, it must be maintained and continually updated on a regular basis. Not only does neglecting diversity hurt the members of the organization, it will lead organizations to lose their competitive edge and allow competitors to gain what only a well-managed, diverse organization can bring.

Although this text was originally developed to help managers become more effective, it is my hope that readers of all educational backgrounds and organizational levels will gain a greater understanding of the benefits of diversity.

I believe that you can make a difference in your organization, no matter what your position is. On a broader scale, I believe it to be better to look at organizations holistically as living and breathing organisms. They are after all, because they are comprised of human beings.

Organizations can be compared to the human body, which is created from millions of living individual cells. When a cell becomes unhealthy due to exposure to toxic elements, it either dies or makes other cells less productive and sick too.

The same can be said of an organization, which atrophies when its members stagnate and do not grow. Therefore, in these toxic circumstances, we must find ways to nurse people back to optimum health, starting in the mind, in order to keep our organizations healthy.

As mentioned, it takes just one person to make a difference in an organization. Perhaps you can be one of those people to actively help others at your place of employment to understand and embrace diversity.

I looking forward to hearing from you about your observations, findings, stories and successes related to using the thoughts about this book. Please contact me through my website: *http://www.paulgerhardt.com* or send me an email: *dr.paul@paulgerhardt.com*.

Thank you.

—Paul L. Gerhardt

CHAPTER ONE

THE BIGGER PICTURE

I define diversity as: *Understanding and utilizing the unique contributions and talents of ALL of an organization's employees—by creating a work environment where everyone is openly invited to be involved.*

Diversity brings valuable new ideas and perspectives to all types of teams. No two people are exactly alike and therefore, it is wrong to assume that even people who have similar physical characteristics will have the same belief systems or talents. Therefore, people who *truly* understand the worth of diversity know that every person deserves to be treated with respect and to be welcomed to contribute ideas with the expectation that those ideas could prove valuable.

Valuing diversity is a way of life for me. I was raised in a multicultural family, work in a multicultural environment, and married into a multicultural family. As a multicultural person, I feel that I have been given the privilege to be able to understand cultural self-awareness from various perspectives. I grew up in a primarily Caucasian small town and thought of myself as Caucasian until I moved to a multicultural major metropolitan city in the early 1990s. I realized that others saw me as different.

However, I have found that I work well with people of diverse backgrounds and have learned to appreciate my own personal background through academic studies and interaction with others of differing backgrounds in my places of employment, education, and in the general public.

In 1997, I had the privilege of attending my first diversity workshop and that year took part in coordinating my own diversity workshop, inviting people from miles around.

Today, I facilitate diversity workshops professionally. I love to help people understand that appreciating cultural self-awareness is about understanding who you are, what your personal background is, and even more importantly, knowing what your personal biases are and how they affect your paradigms, which influence how you act toward others.

As a leader, teacher, and community member, I get the opportunity to work with people of numerous cultural backgrounds. I consciously show each person that I value their diversity and similarities on an individual basis. I appreciate the richness of life that diversity brings to organizations and do my best at helping others feel comfortable with diversity, too.

I wrote this book to help people at all levels in an organization to understand how to be more effective in the workplace and in their own personal lives. Although much of what I have written deals with the responsibilities of human resource professionals and upper level managers in terms of managing diversity, I believe that any person, no matter what his/her job title, can influence the organization in a positive way.

I thoroughly believe that business is only *secondarily* about products or services. All business is *primarily* about the people in each organization—both customers and employees, who either directly or indirectly serve the customers. I believe that if everyone within an organization maintains this principle in their hearts and minds, workplaces will quickly become places where people love to work and customers love to frequent. Moreover, satisfied customers will recommend the business to their friends and family.

As a consultant and author, I believe I have a responsibility to share what I have learned to make the world a little easier and a generally better place to live. Toward that end, this text sheds some light on how to become more effective in the workplace and in life in general. Since (on average) at least one-third of our lives take place at work, creating a working environment that people enjoy is essential.

Diversity is present in all areas of public life. Therefore, if we can learn to be effective leaders, we can make the most from what we have. It takes personal leadership for us to become much closer to each other, but we can also learn to understand who we are as individuals from diversity initiatives.

The Secret of Effective Leadership Starts with You

One of the greatest motivation researchers of all time, Abraham Maslow, suggested that people can do their best work when they have attained self-actualization. Maslow's definition of self-actualization includes realizing one's own personal potential and finding self-fulfillment. Although many of us believe we are self-actualized, most of us are only scraping the surface of who we truly are. We have no idea what we can accomplish and what our true individual potential can be. Maslow takes the premise one more level, believing that once we reach self-actualization, we will be further enhanced by helping others reach that level.

I believe that self-actualization can only be possible when we create opportunities for personal-growth—derived through paradigm shifts in our thinking. Since we have only the lenses of our own eyes that create our perception of our own reality, we must proactively broaden our personal understanding through continual education. This can be done most optimally when we open up our lives to others' ideas and perceptions.

Formalized training and education are just a couple varieties of education that yield personal growth. Books, audio CDs, videos, and other similar media that are geared toward personal enhancement should also be a consistent part of your daily life. As busy as our lives are, taking the time to enrich our minds with growth-oriented media will help us become more organized in every human encounter.

Creating Relationships that Matter

As a human race, we must learn to build trusting relationships with people of all backgrounds. We must be open to the potential growth that may result from close, personal conversations and time spent with every person whom we come in contact. Through new technologies, the world is getting smaller and smaller. Rather than seeing the glass as half-empty and focusing on the world getting more crowded, we must learn to see the glass as half-full and to notice that we have more opportunities to gain new friends or close-colleagues and to enrich our lives with new ideas from others.

Furthermore, one cannot ignore that every country is becoming a mosaic of multiculturalism. Every organization must fully realize what this means. After studying this text, hopefully you will better understand that diversity not only *needs to be understood, but it also must be actively embraced.* The first organizations to do this fully will gain a competitive edge over the competition for reasons described hereafter.

Someday, in the near future, all existing organizations will be multicultural, ideally reflecting the communities they serve. For this very reason, diversity programs must not be just "programs." They must become deeply ingrained in the foundations of the organization's systems, practices, policies, procedures, marketing, and production.

Recommendations for helping diversity programs to succeed, as well as how to implement necessary organizational change are outlined in detail further in this book. Readers will gain a deeper understanding of what multiculturalism is all about and be given tools to help individuals examine their personal values and beliefs. Analyzing and adjusting values, beliefs, as well as personal biases are the *most important* aspects of making diversity work both personally and professionally.

There truly is enough success available in this world for everyone. However, it must be sought out, as a fisherman seeks an abundant catch. Fish do not jump into boats; they must be taken from the sea with the proper equipment, skill, and training. It is my hope that this book serves not only as a tool for personal development, but also as a reference for continual use. I am excited about the futures in store for people when they gain a better understanding of diversity.

Please allow yourself the opportunity to explore what you currently know, and also to let go of unnecessary understandings. Be free to question what you already know and consider this book with an open mind.

Being a leader is not about having a title that says Manager, Director, or Vice President; it is about having integrity in both actions and words. It is about helping other people self-actualize. It is about you mastering knowledge and personal abilities.

I hope this book helps readers to move forward in their lives with the invigorated integrity of true leadership. Life is so much more fulfilling when we live it in a way that is truly authentic. We must uncover and learn what our potentials are. When we know what they are, we can then take them to new levels and help others do the same.

CHAPTER TWO

IMPORTANCE OF DIVERSITY

Organizational diversity is important for three primary reasons: law, ethics, and business practice. Every person with management responsibility must be aware of their legal duties. Failing to do so may be costly. Discrimination lawsuits take valuable time, cost a great deal of money, and even worse, creates bad publicity that only time and well-planned measures can heal.

It is far less expensive for businesses to properly establish diversity programs that create environments where people feel they are being treated fairly. Even more so, companies may find it quite profitable to continually educate their employees. Properly implemented diversity programs help to continually monitor progress of sales and profits when the employee base reflects the communities and clientele that they wish to serve.

Multicultural understanding, derived through diversity training programs translate into organizational success and individual fulfillment gained through personal growth. Diversity, when properly managed, can increase sales, productivity and revenues, which are the signs of healthy organizations.

Test my theory about healthy organizations, characterized by employees who are most productive. Maximized productivity comes as a result of people feeling that they are an important part of a company that truly values them as individuals.

What Effective Diversity Looks Like

Successful diversity programs should typically ensure that managerial employees at all levels do not have the same backgrounds. Ideally, an even number of men, women, and people of color should report to next-level managers. Effective organizational multiculturalism is typically depicted when managerial-level employees lead people who reflect the customers or potential make-up of the consumers they wish to serve. In other words, the managers must look like the customers (or potential customers) and many of the employees should look like the customers, too. When this happens, employees will have a better understanding of how to best serve people.

Managers should be actively serving the employees they lead. They should be providing proper resources for their followers' and remove any obstacles that impede progress. Workers who are directly serving customers should be empowered to use their knowledge of the business and culture to anticipate customer desires and needs. Employees at other levels of the organization should also be empowered to use their knowledge of their coworkers, based on job knowledge and cultural familiarity.

Testing the Health of Organizations

When interacting with a company or organization that you deal with, take some time to investigate how truly happy the employees are. Don't just stop by asking one employee if he or she is happy with the employer. Try to find several other employees who will take the time and be honest with you. Not all employees are willing to trust you enough to be honest with you. You may need to find an approach that works best for you in order to get a clearer picture about the organization as a whole.

People generally will be honest about their feelings when they are shown that the other person conveys trustworthiness, through both actions and words. Some people, of course, will not trust others due to previous experiences that compromise their ability to trust. You will know in your heart and gut if you are getting an honest answer. We always do. However, many of us have learned to ignore our gut instincts because they seem less than scientific or impractical.

In the words of the famous popular shoe pitchman—Michael Jordan, "Just Do It!" You will find that you are usually right most of the time. Most likely, you have only learned to practice not trusting your instincts. We of course, can learn to unlearn poor beliefs and learn good ones. A wise person once wrote, "We practice who we are and practice makes us who we are."

Take some time to take the test. You will know an employee who seems happy in her job when you see someone who goes that extra mile. Ask her about what she likes about the job. Come back later and try talking to somebody else. See if it was a fluke that you found someone who appeared to love the company she works for. If it seems that most employees love the organization, take a moment to observe what the employees look like. You may see that such happy organizations have people from many different cultural backgrounds in management and working at all levels.

When employees are happy, the organization is healthy. When the organization is healthy, it is characteristically looking for further opportunities for growth and enhancing sales revenues, product lines, or services.

The opposite is also very true. I can always tell when an organization has at least one manager somewhere within the organization who is failing to be a good leader. Such leaders create systems and interact in ways that hinder organizational success. As a result, these organizations are filled with good employees who will not go that extra mile, because they are frustrated by being held back from working optimally or delivering the best service or productivity they can.

Employees led by poor leaders generally do not smile much. If they do, it is forced because it is expected of them. Poor leadership is often characterized by subordinates doing only the minimum of what they have to do, rather than what needs to be done.

Employees working under poor leaders will do what needs to be done when people are looking. When no one is around, their productivity often suffers.

Effective Leadership and Motivation

I agree with the late, great father of management science, W. E. Deming. He argued that when things do not happen as they need to; the systems (leadership included) are more at fault than the employees involved.

People are motivated through empowerment, trust, and respect. They need to be given the proper tools, equipment, and resources to make things happen. Motivation for future action is reinforced when employees are recognized both publicly (in front of peers) and privately on a regular basis (at least once a week) for benefiting the organization. Recognition only provides value when it is received as genuine and is specifically directed toward a behavior that should be repeated. Poor leaders fail to provide proper recognition consistently, as their jobs should mandate. If you are a leader, make sure that you praise your subordinates minimally once a week for specific accomplishments that were done well.

Here is how it works: A vicious cycle is created. First, a worker does exceptional work, but is not recognized for doing it. This perpetuates poor leadership as a result of employees not finding the needed motivation to continue to deliver exceptional work. This in turn makes the leader not want to recognize what he believes his employees should accomplish. Nobody is happy in this common workplace scenario.

This vicious cycle could be stopped by leaders, who must first change their patterns of not recognizing and praising good work habits.

Even the tiniest of accomplishments should be praised. The praise should be genuine and come from the heart. It should be expressed with words the receiver will understand and value. The praise should be specifically directed to a particular occurrence and not just, *"Good job today!"* Rather, it should be more like, "I heard how you went the extra mile for Mr. Rodriguez. I am impressed! Thank you!"

Such practices of genuine appreciation will go a long way, especially if they are practiced regularly. Effective leaders praise and thank employees for specific jobs they have witnessed done well, authentically, often and regularly.

Diversity, Communication, and Training

It is important to note that just because an organization has done a good job hiring a culturally diverse staff, it might still do a poor job managing employee morale. Organizations must invest in continual training dealing with leadership, diversity, and team-building.

Employees need to be placed in jobs that fit their skill sets, interests, and abilities to learn the job. Training is a vital component of successful organizations and must be followed-up on to make sure that all employees know what is expected of them and therefore they are performing their work in an acceptable way.

I have trained employees of diverse cultural backgrounds whose second language was English. Some have assured me that they understood the expectations, but did not. Later I found that they learned that it was easier just to say they understood and try to figure out what to do on their own. Often this results in failure.

Of course, if communication that simply leaves a message with the recipient, who is not understanding it, this is not communication at all. This is simply one person talking.

Therefore, trainees should be asked to repeat the expectations in a way that the trainer knows they have a mutual understanding. The most effective trainers go as far as to watch the employees perform the expected tasks and encourage them to ask any questions they may have. Keep in mind that great trainers help employees see how every function expected of them will specifically affect the total operation of the organization, as well as how it contributes to overall company operation success.

The Greatest Motivator

My favorite business story illustrates how communicating the "bigger picture of the task" is a crucial component to motivation. I was told this story by a friend, while I worked on my doctorate. This story is about two CEOs of rival companies who argued whether money was the greatest motivator for people. You may be surprised to learn the outcome.

As the story goes, the CEO of a company (we'll call it X Company) bet the CEO of the other company (Y Company) that money was the greatest motivator for employees. "The more you pay an employee, the happier the employee is and therefore will do anything to get the job done and do their best at it."

The CEO of Y Company did not agree and took the bet of the CEO of X Company. They agreed that they could come to a conclusion by hiring someone to do a job of no significance and no contribution to the organization.

Together, the two CEOs found a homeless man on the street and offered him the meaningless job of digging a hole of specific dimensions—one-foot by one-foot. After the hole was completed it was to then to be refilled. This job was to take place over and over—forty hours each week and eight hours every day. The contract also specified that the hole needed to be done precisely as they specified. He could not use any other tools than those provided for him, and he could not deviate from the terms of the contract. Simply put, he needed to do exactly what was asked of him. Nothing more. Nothing less. And with no further communication.

The job sounded easy enough to the homeless man who was excited about the opportunity to earn a relatively quick fortune. They signed a contract with the man, specifying that if he did this job for one month, he would receive $100,000. If he failed to complete the month, he would get nothing.

The man agreed and started his new job that day. It took only three hours of digging and refilling the hole before the man walked off the job. He broke his contract and did not receive any compensation.

When both CEOs heard that the man quit on the first day, the two CEOs reconvened.

One CEO argued that he did not find the right person for the job and that they should try it again with someone who was an experienced ditch digger. So, the very next day, they went out and found a professional and experienced ditch digger. They asked this man if he was interested in doing the very same insignificant task. They specified that the job had no considerable contribution to either of their organizations.

Again the contract was quickly signed under the same conditions as it was with the homeless man. This time the professional ditch digger lasted only a few hours of doing the work and walked off the job without pay.

The CEO who bet that money was the greatest motivator acquiesced to his adversary and sorrowfully paid his debt. Both CEOs then began the task of making sure that every employee could see how their jobs contributed to the overall success of their respective organizations.

Managerial Secrets of Success

When managers understand how to be effective leaders, employees feel like they are valued and empowered to make the best decisions for the organization. Effective leadership helps individuals to be themselves and cultivates their individual talents in order to benefit the organization. People must understand how their contributions benefit the organizations in order to gain both personal fulfillment and job satisfaction.

From a multicultural perspective, mangers need to find the most qualified person for every job. With this in mind, when that applicant is a person of color and reflects the people they serve, it is even better. As often stated, people like to associate with those who look like them. People simply feel more comfortable and less threatened in these cases.

The old-fashioned model of having managers fit a "traditional look" of a manager—a tall, blonde, White, male does not lay a foundation for creating and maintaining the most effective organizations anymore. The most progressive organizations hire and promote women and people of color to fill valuable leadership roles.

When employees at lower levels of the organization see such diversity, their motivation and morale are improved greatly. More often than not, employees are inspired by believing that they can be promoted to positions of greater responsibility and peer acceptance, rather than being led to believe that only White men will fill these roles. This has traditionally been the case.

CHAPTER THREE

ETHICS AND BUSINESS

From an ethical perspective, both individuals and organizations can benefit from developing values that employ diversity thinking. Sound ethical practices are a fundamental part of doing business and are also a necessity for effective win-win human interaction. Dr. Stephen R. Covey discusses this aspect more in his best-selling book, *Seven Habits of Highly Effective People.*

Employers should know that potential new employees may base their decision of employment on perceived organizational culture. The workforce is shrinking due to the requirements of increased production needs and the availability of people with the "right stuff" to fill the job requirements. Therefore, the job market is becoming quite competitive.

Organizations require employees with the talent, knowledge, and experience to maintain their organization's health and competitiveness. Creating an ethical culture may be the difference in hiring a talented employee and investing in training her, versus losing her and her valuable experience to a competitor.

Outrageous Costs of Doing Business

Costs associated with filling job vacancies are quickly becoming one of the highest expenses in business. Time, of course, translates into money paid to Human Resources professionals for developing job descriptions, advertising available positions, screening job applications, interviewing, and conducting personnel background checks. Other expenses related to filling a vacancy go into training.

On average, it takes two years for an employee to become fully trained and competent in all work-duties. This means that in order for a new employee to do the work of his predecessor, costly mistakes will be made and production capacity will be delayed until he acquires the practice and repetition it takes to become competent at a job.

Research suggests that, on average, it takes over $35,000 to hire and fully train a new employee. This is much more expensive than developing a work culture where people want to do their best and never want to leave their jobs, which naturally lowers the cost of doing business. The money that once went into recruitment and training can then be put to better use for the company.

Of course, the costs associated with losing an employee to a competitor are immeasurable. It is very difficult to quantify how much revenue, production, or other losses can be attributed to an employee who leaves and takes her talents, experience, competency, and loyal customers with her.

Therefore, effective leaders must understand that managing an organization is both an art and science. Business is about people first and then about the products and services. Leaders, no matter what title they hold, need to live this philosophy or expect to perish professionally.

Diversity-Thinking and Loyal Membership

Making employees feel valued and secure in their jobs is much more crucial than ever before. Understanding and employing the rules of diversity-thinking is tantamount to being an effective leader. It is also very important in creating an organization characterized by both loyal employees and customers.

Diversity-thinking employs the philosophy that every employee has the potential to bring exceptional value to the organization and should be nurtured to do so. Again, this equates to effective communication. Employees should have plenty of opportunities to ask questions and for leaders to do the same.

Leading in Communication

The organizations' communication arena must always be fluidly open. Leaders must be socially conscious when it comes to hearing the true message of what each speaker is trying to convey. Likewise, the receiver of the message must be able to aptly confirm that she understands the message. This is often done effectively by repeating what she has heard. Even better, she should repeat it in her own words (paraphrasing) for clarification.

Effective leaders must also be aware that healthy communication fosters healthy relationships. Leaders lose their power when subordinates lose respect for them because they perceive the leader is insincere, unethical, or unwilling to reciprocate an opportunity to listen.

Likewise, valuable, effective communication can be stifled when the leader shuts down an employee by not hearing or truly considering what he is attempting to share. Leaders must always take the time to stop what they are doing, show that they are listening, and show that they are giving respectful consideration for the information the subordinate is sharing.

Leadership Rights and Wrongs

Leaders should always tell the truth and should not misrepresent anything. Just as important, leaders should never make off-handed comments or jokes about any person's ethnicity, background, or appearance. This lack of professionalism, no matter how innocent, may be construed as lack of character, or as racism or bigotry. Such comments are never appropriate in the workplace or outside the work arena.

If a person thinks that she is being appropriate or funny with such casual comments, I highly recommend that this individual should consider the consequences of losing the respect of others. Followers will quickly wonder what is being said about them behind their backs. Trust will be diminished by the followers and leadership power is virtually dissolved.

On the other hand, giving credit to subordinates when ideas come to fruition is an effective way to keep valuable ideas flowing. This also enhances the competitiveness of the organization. Effective leaders always find ways to praise!

Failing to give credit to subordinates, shutting employees down, not listening, or belittling them will directly have the opposite effect. In the long run, leaders who practice poor communication will become ineffective and eventually lose credibility. Therefore, lose the power to lead.

Teams, Insight and Values

Effective leaders who utilize diversity thinking realize that in today's competitive world, building teams of homogenous "yes-men" could mean death to success. Diversity brings strength in differences of opinions. This translates to avoiding costly mistakes that were foreseen only by employees who understand other possible components or outcomes from decisions.

Diversity brings insight about ideas, which will help meet the desires of customers through changes to products or services. This, in turn, will help make the organization more competitive by appealing to certain diversity groups. Therefore, employees must be empowered to share their ideas openly and often.

Employing ethical values that consider diversity issues can give an organization the competitive-edge they are looking for. People of all backgrounds wish to be treated with dignity and respect. Ethical values that are reflected in business practices yield greater results in the long run than organizations that act unethically by misleading customers and employees. This means they should be honest at all times and never mislead anyone or show favoritism to any person over another.

As mentioned earlier, wise human resource managers know that it is much more costly to replace an existing employee than it is to recruit, hire, and train a new one. Some of the costs indirectly associated with losing an existing employee, which must be considered, come from the potential loss of future customers' business, when they were more loyal to the lost employee than to the company. These costs are difficult to measure precisely, but customer defection, according to some studies is estimated to be the equivalent of more than half of an operation's annual revenues.

Food for Thought

It is well known among marketing professionals that organizations are required to advertise and market their company's products and services in order to be competitive. One primary reason is the need to replenish the valuable supply of lost customers. Customers tend to patronize organizations that give them what they expect and treat them as they wish to be treated. This is sometimes referred to as, *"The Platinum Rule of Diversity."*

The most powerful form of advertisement occurs by word-of-mouth through completely-satisfied customers. In order to completely satisfy a customer, the organization must act ethically with its employees. By doing so, it lessens the possibility that employees will purposefully fail to act in the best interest to a company that slighted them. Every employee is a diplomat for their company. *In the eyes of their customers, they are the company.*

The same is also true for employees. If employees are expected to act in an ethical way toward customers, they must always practice integrity. Leaders must encourage integrity in everything they say and do. Leaders must treat employees as they wish their employees to treat their customers.

As the saying goes, *effective leaders "must do as they say and say as they do."* Effective leaders cannot waiver at all in this practice and risk losing the respect of their followers. This is what integrity is all about. Leadership research heavily indicates that the most-effective leaders share integrity as one of their greatest strengths.

Integrity is also the most-requested characteristic of followers.

Trust, Lies, Power, and Vicious Circles

Leaders lose power when they fail to follow through on what they are going to do or act in a way that can be perceived as unethical. Followers have every reason to begin talking with each other about the failings of their leaders. A vicious circle characterized by a lack of trust between leader and followers begins from employees' doubting their leaders' integrity. In such situations, it is difficult for leaders to recover their lost power. Only time and consistent acts of integrity can slowly revive such fallen leaders.

Similarly, it is difficult to win back the business of dissatisfied customers who feel they were not treated as they expected. It is even more difficult when they are treated in an unethical way. Another vicious cycle, similar to that of the leader and the disgruntled employees can begin. Dissatisfied customers will use their powerful right of self-expression with friends and family, which can quickly erode the reputation and good-standing of any organization.

On the other hand, when satisfied customers tell friends or family members about their positive experiences with an organization, the results can be quite dynamic. The existing trust between them endorses the company in a most powerful way. In turn, the friends or family members will share what they have learned about the company, product, or service with others. Before long, satisfied customers become valuable unpaid marketing members of the organization by selling the value of the organization to (potentially) hundreds of people.

The Psychology of it All

Positive psychological connections are naturally created to products and services. People find it unsurprisingly easy to make purchases if it helps fill a void in their personal need for peer validation and social recognition. This can occur as a direct result of the knowledge that social members or often respected celebrities endorse certain products. As a result, purchasers feel better off for buying or association.

The converse is also very true. It is human nature for people to seek satisfaction. When customers become dissatisfied with a product, service, or company, they tend to do the opposite as in a positive experience, and the outcome is much worse for companies in question.

Research shows that unsatisfied customers tend to seek vengeance by publicly telling far more than just a handful of people about their negative experiences. This negative publicity is powerfully destructive to the organization's reputation and revenues. It therefore becomes necessary for organizations to budget huge portions of their income for marketing campaigns developed to win back customers and find new ones to replace the ones they lost.

Technology, Leadership, and Character

Contemporary business is no longer dictated by location and price, as in the past. Technology has opened the marketplace on a global scale. Products can be produced and obtained from anywhere, which brings prices down due to the diversity of global wage tiers and the associated costs of production.

Technology makes it possible to get almost anything one desires. With a couple clicks of a button and next-day delivery, competition runs rampant. Today's business professional must concentrate on customer service, value, and selection, as well as practicing integrity in every human interaction.

When mistakes happen, wise leaders take responsibility for the mishap and do whatever it takes to win back the trust of the follower or customer. Every person makes mistakes, but it takes character to admit to making mistakes. Likewise, learning from mistakes builds character and helps others through example to do the same.

Character, Integrity, and Fixing What Is Wrong

One of my favorite business stories that best illustrates the fundamental relationship between ethical business practices and the fragile relationship that customers have with organizations. This is a great one for every leader to ponder. I love to share this story with my students and clients. It is a powerful tale of a restaurant and a shrewd businessman.

One day a man and his bride were driving down a coastal highway to a bed and breakfast on their honeymoon in a town many miles from where they were married. On the way to their honeymoon destination, the couple had conversations of how wonderful their life together would be. They discussed their hopes, dreams, and common interests.

They soon realized that they both loved to cook and that they should soon start their life in a new town that would give them both a fresh new start. The conversations were filled with many ideas and a lot of love.

The couple discussed the cuisine they would serve and what the restaurant would look like. In these moments of synergy during their honeymoon (enhanced by their profound passion for each other), the couple worked out all the details in their plans for their business. This is a true indication of what synergy can do.

As luck would have it, their honeymoon destination was a town with only a couple of places to eat. To them, this was a sure sign that their restaurant was meant to be. They knew that in order to make their dreams a reality they would have to wait and save their pennies.

In the following years, the couple had saved enough money to open their restaurant. They renovated an old retail location on the waterfront of the same town where they honeymooned. The couple hired the friendliest staff from the town and created some of the tastiest seafood dishes. They quickly developed a reputation for having the best customer service and the best food in the state.

Their biggest draw was their signature seafood chowder. They used the creamiest cream and the most buttery butter. They included nine varieties of seafood and only the freshest assortment of hand-picked herbs and vine-ripened vegetables. Newspapers' culinary columns would consistently give rave reviews of the restaurant. Of course, word quickly spread about the couple's delicious seafood chowder, and people came from all over the world just to enjoy it.

Business flourished and the couple soon had to expand the size of the building. They eventually bought nearly all of the property on their block to meet the increasing demands of their business. They hired more staff and paid them well. They encouraged and empowered their employees to do whatever it took to satisfy and exceed their customers' expectations. They let the staff wear whatever they wanted to wear with the only stipulations that it be clean and professional.

The couple was amazed on what a success they had become in relatively such a short period of time. They found that by giving their customers the very best and by treating every customer as a valued guest, they would never have to fear going out of business. People had to make reservations weeks in advance, because the restaurant was always packed.

One day a shrewd businessman came to town to taste the legendary chowder and indulge in the renowned hospitality of the owners and employees. The business man loved the restaurant so much that he quickly offered to buy it. Reluctantly, the owners were convinced to sell their business, but they only agreed to the deal after they were offered enough to retire comfortably.

The shrewd businessman had to take out a second mortgage on his lavish home and convince a few investors to loan him the money needed to make the deal. He was now heavily in debt, but believed that he could do better than the previous owners at making his fortune.

The new owner of the restaurant immediately began to look for ways to cut costs. He fired some of the staff that had been working at the restaurant since it had opened because he believed they had been paid too much. Besides, the staff that remained could work a little harder and still get the job done. On top of this, he chose a new dress code for everyone. It now required his approval to wear anything different. The staff hated the new uniforms and thought they were ugly. This was only the beginning.

He reevaluated the ingredients of the cuisine and quickly began to make substitutions with less expensive items. In their signature chowder, he substituted milk for the cream and margarine for the butter. He discontinued some of the nine varieties of seafood in the chowder and settled on using only four. He also stopped using fresh herbs and vegetables and substituted dried and previously frozen ones, which were much cheaper.

Local customers immediately noticed the difference and stopped coming. They felt betrayed for losing the service and quality they had come to expect. The media stopped writing rave reviews about the service, staff, and food. Most of the original staff was gone and the remaining ones were fearful of their new owner and the possibility that they too might lose their jobs.

The quality of the service and food had diminished. Not only did people stop coming from miles around, but the locals stopped coming as well. Business was dying.

Eventually, the shrewd businessman was no longer able to pay the restaurant's mortgage and bills. Only a couple months after he took over the business, he was forced to close the doors and declare bankruptcy.

Many business lessons can be learned from the story of the restaurant. Lessons about diversity have the same theme of treating people in a way in which they want to be treated. Including existing members organizations, no matter what their background, in decision-making processes is crucial. Diversity of thoughts leads to many more ideas to derive success through. As a general rule, always give people your very best and never skimp on it.

The Platinum Rule of Diversity Thinking

One of the most powerful laws of diversity thinking is ethical by nature. It dictates, "Treat people as they wish to be treated." It is the platinum rule of diversity and is closely-related to the golden rule, "Treat others as you wish to be treated."

Diversity thinking acknowledges and accounts for differences in every individual and is ethical in nature because it pertains to decision-making and action. Diversity thinking promotes the philosophy that every person has the right to be who they wish to be. People should not be judged adversely for being who they want to be, as long as they are not harming others, nor infringing on the rights of others.

This fact is especially understood by effective leaders who wish to continue doing business by creating an environment where employees are happy and content. In turn, this makes customers more motivated to keep coming back.

More about Diversity Thinking and Customers

Customers are the primary external source that feeds every organization, but they are not the property of any organization. They are rarely loyal to organizations that act unethically with them or fail to meet their expectations. When customers defect, organizations become less competitive and often perish.

Therefore, I will say it again: more often than not, employees who feel that they are being treated ethically and fairly will treat customers the same way. In turn, customers will remember how they were treated and will have less reason to consider discontinuing the business relationship.

The management *theory of expectancy* suggests that employees will get what they believe they are owed. If they are treated poorly, they will do what they feel will compensate for it. This includes stealing or sabotaging the business' success. Diversity thinking aligns with the expectancy theory by suggesting that actions must be ethically sound. People must be treated fairly according to personal expectations. People are motivated through the expectation that they will be rewarded appropriately and treated fairly as they see others in the organization being treated. Leaders should never forget about this value found in the management theory of expectancy.

Effective leaders must treat customers and employees with individual respect. They can do this by identifying the expectations of both groups, so that they may meet those expectations. As a result, employees will act according to what they believe is correct. As an added bonus, customers will feel contentment.

Demographics and Doing Business

Finally, from a business viewpoint, it makes good sense to recognize changes in the demographics of those to whom the organization caters. Likewise, decision-makers in organizations should analyze their workforce and see if it represents those they serve, meaning their customers. Companies that take advantage of this general guideline will have the opportunity to increase sales, gain new ideas, and have a better future overall.

In these competitive times, organizations need to be smart in the way they hire, implement policies, and conduct business. In order for organizations to maximize their success, diversity should be a conscious, foundational cornerstone in every aspect of their business.

Successfully implemented diversity programs have been shown to enhance every aspect of the organizations in which they are properly placed. If your organization needs help, there are professionals who can make that difference. Diversity experts can be hired to evaluate competitive factors, as they pertain to diversity. Programs must be put into place, continually evaluated, and reevaluated for success. Once a diversity program is fully functioning, the organization can operate with many new benefits.

Research shows that there are numerous organizational benefits for effective diversity programs. Some of the benefits include reducing employee turnover and its costs, reducing absenteeism, and acquisition of new resources by attracting the best personnel as the labor pool changes and shrinks. Properly working diversity programs bring insight and cultural sensitivity to the marketing effort.

CHAPTER FOUR

SUCCESS FACTORS
OF DIVERSITY

As discussed earlier in this book, programs that instill diversity thinking and practices in organizations must be fully supported by the organization's management team. That means that every person who holds responsibility for managing others must also be leaders in diversity thinking. These leaders must be educated in diversity philosophy and must truly see the value of diversity thinking. All leaders must be sensitive to the needs of their subordinates and do what it takes to help organizational members support diversity initiatives. These leaders must be challenged to understand their own personal biases and evaluate their own values.

Once a management team takes personal ownership for leading the diversity program, it must understand that this program needs to be permanent and not just come and go, as so many programs often do.

Keeping a Diversity Program Alive

Diversity programs need to be living and breathing; they need to be seen as the lifeblood of the organization. As with any program, the crucial aspect of communication is tantamount and should be practiced regularly. Organizational leaders must never speak ill of the diversity program and must truly believe that promoting diversity is the right thing to do. Furthermore, effective leaders must encourage others to promote diversity thinking often and truly listen to what others are saying.

As with any important organizational initiative, diversity thinking must be regularly promoted in daily discussions among subordinates and peers. The conversations need to be more than company lip-service; they must acknowledge the positive contributions that are being made by others who are actively embracing diversity thinking. People must be genuinely and publicly praised for their contributions in the name of diversity. Likewise, when others may reject diversity initiatives, they must be privately counseled and brought back on board.

Helping others support diversity initiatives can be challenging. It takes skillful consideration and excellent listening skills. For some, it may mean painting a picture that changes the heart of someone who resents diversity thinking. In most cases, people who do not support diversity thinking hold personal biases brought on by past experiences, which misguide their decision-making processes. These biases may be very strong and seem to be a part of their personality because they may have learned to love having these biases. Worse yet, others may encourage and praise such negative beliefs. If unable to come around to the bigger picture of diversity thinking, these people may need to be let go.

One of the most important practices that an effective leader must execute is to surround himself with the most talented people. These people must be dedicated to making the needed changes to support and develop their organization's initiatives. They need to find ways to incorporate the initiatives into their daily routines and at the same time; skillfully include their own personality and work ideas to help it thrive.

Communicating diversity thinking takes education. The educational process must delve into each individual's belief systems. People must have a clear understanding of why diversity is important to the organization's success and see how they play a major part in that vision of success. More about the communication and education processes will be covered later in this book. Communication, as it relates to education is the single most important aspect of developing an organization that embraces diversity.

Organizational Change

Implementing change through education will also create a successful diversity thinking-driven program. Organizational change is one of the biggest challenges leaders face because many members of an organization tend to fear change. Most people find it easier to embrace what is comfortable, no matter if it works effectively or not. Change represents venturing into the unknown. Many people become accustomed to coping within effective organizational systems and would rather not waste energy trying to make them work. That energy needs to be skillfully redirected to create and implement programs that do work. It is the leader's job to help the "change-resister." She needs to see that the changes are both necessary and can work. She needs to understand that her role in the process is vital. Effective leaders who are skilled at implementing organizational change know that the first step is helping others to see the need for the change. Part of this process is acknowledging and honoring past ways of doing things.

When someone passes away, friends and relatives often go through a denial phase and only eventually reach acceptance. This usually does not happen overnight, but occurs through a gradual period of time. Diversity programs must be accepted by every member and eventually embraced. Most organizations cannot afford to have even one member dragging their heels. Everyone must be encouraged to embrace change through an educational process. Somehow, resisters must be helped to come to the conclusion that their non-supportive attitude adversely affects the progress of the organization. Organizational leaders must evaluate every situation and determine whether or not such an employee is bringing value to the organization or holding the organization back. After doing this, leaders must make the best decision for the company and the individual.

Acceptance, Change, and Synergy

Every stage of change must be supported by genuine appreciation toward those who embrace the change through consistent words of affirmation. Effective leaders understand the psychological need for acceptance and praise because they know that it reinforces that followers should continue to do the right thing.

When change involves diversity thinking, every organizational member must come to the conclusion that diversity leads to fueling creative synergy. Synergy is the maximized outcome that is greater than the sum of its parts. When people are doing their own thing and producing results, their actions must be tied to a single vision. People must be encouraged to openly share their ideas and know how they can support the greater vision.

Diversity thinking focuses on the people involved—both the employees and customers. The associated costs must not be the primary drivers, but builders of revenue—creating added value for all involved. As noted, diversity thinking in business is the realization that business concerns people first, and products and services secondarily.

The Secrets to Successful Change

When people work for the sake of building positive relationships, revenues soon follow. Relationships and revenues go hand-in-hand. When businesses fixate on costs and revenues alone, the people-aspect is diminished, leaving an opening for competitors to fill that valuable niche.

Change is best implemented when performance measures are used. All members of the organization must know what the vision is and have attainable goals that outline a roadmap to success. When each of the goals is accomplished, it must be reinforced with praise and celebration. These can come in the form of formalized rewards, bonuses, or symbolized gifts of appreciation, like certificates presented to followers in the presence of their peers. Each milestone reached must be recognized as progress toward accomplishing the final goal. These steps must be attainable, measurable, and realistic. Failing to meet these basic needs will only inhibit future progress.

Change leaders must make sure that subordinates have the proper tools, resources, and technology to accomplish their goals. Employees who are frustrated because they are doing the best they can, but do not have adequate resources to make it happen often take one step forward and several steps backward. When this happens, leaders often unknowingly sabotage the progression of change. They discipline the employee or employees involved, rather than address the real problem—the systems and resources.

W.E. Deming, father of management science, suggests that people typically amount to only 5% of the problem. The remaining 95% of an organization's problems are typically attributable to the systems in which the people work. This philosophy aligns closely to diversity thinking.

People generally want to do the right thing and to seek success. Putting the right people, systems, and resources in place is fundamental for organizational success.

When processes are redesigned to align with an organizational vision that incorporates diversity thinking, jobs and procedures must also be changed. Effective leaders must take an active role in training employees in their new roles and remove any barriers that impede or restrict the successful change. All change must be tied to the existing organizational culture when making necessary changes. This is especially true when the goal is to change the culture.

The Art of Leading Change and the Dance of Power

As suggested earlier, leaders must make sure that they have the right people in the right places according to talents and experience. If people are not accomplishing the goals they set in partnership with their leaders, those people may need to be replaced by someone who better matches the task requirements and is willing to do what it takes to get the job done.

Effective leaders must make this type of employee change in a tactful way, preserving every person's dignity. Onlookers constantly judge leaders by their actions, and leaders must be consciously aware of it. Leaders must also realize that their effectiveness and power comes primarily from their followers. Once respect from the followers is lost because they are fearful of a leader, it is difficult to regain.

Leaders implementing any type of change must always be evaluating every level of the organization for consensus. This can best be accomplished by means of frank conversations with key members of teams. It is important for leaders to practice effective listening and to make clarification of what they are hearing, in order to assess what needs to take place, if anything. Questions should be directed by identifying team members' feelings and determining that they have adequate resources to accomplish their tasks. Do the members of the organization really believe that change is necessary, or do they believe it is just "*another HR initiative?*" Leaders need to focus on integrity and honesty in their dealings with each employee. Listening may be the primer needed to motivate others to be successful in accomplishing their tasks.

Leaders may need to take steps to change milestones or if desired results are not achieved. Involving key people in evaluating consensus and success is a crucial component of facilitating change. The messages—both verbal and written— must always be consistent and supported by all key people involved. As mentioned earlier, organizational members will best embrace change if they feel that there is value in it. Effective leaders who promote diversity thinking must be skilled at painting pictures of desired outcomes by communicating in a way those followers can comprehend and believe.

If followers speak different languages, interpreters may need to be employed. Finding ways to understand everyone's thoughts, feelings and ideas should be the number one task of a leader. Being heard and understood is like gold to organizational members. It is a natural law that leaders must listen first and then make themselves understood. Interpreters may be the key to making this happen most-effectively.

Followers must know that they have the full backing of their leaders. They must whole heartedly believe that the changes are not only vital, but also realistic and attainable.

The Power of Diversity Thinking

Diversity thinking promotes the philosophy that organizations are more productive and effective when people of differing backgrounds are utilized in areas that draw on their skill and knowledge bases, particularly by placing them in positions to make decisions. This will bring fresh concepts to work teams and improve their abilities to solve problems.

Diversity thinking helps others realize that profits will increase through the kind of synergy that effective diversity programs promote. Organizations that implement diversity programs discover that they not only contribute to social responsibility, which enhances the image of the organization, but also helps increase market share on a local and global scale.

Properly implemented diversity programs improve the quality of management and help others see that it is possible to be promoted, no matter what their background is. Managers of diverse backgrounds aid in solving problems and contribute powerfully-innovating thoughts that lend a hand to the organization's advancement. This, in turn, has a positive effect on increasing productivity and organizational flexibility.

Increased organizational flexibility is derived from companies that team up to form alliances and pool resources to tighten relationships with suppliers and customers. This broadens the scope of potential clientele and helps build a positive reputation in multiple marketing areas.

In addition, leaders who use diversity thinking are characterized by being flexible in meeting the needs of employees and always show respect for every individual. Their flexibility leads employees more effectively and inspires them to be more loyal to their companies. Loyal employees generally look for opportunities to contribute and further the success of their organizations.

Business leaders must always look for ways to increase revenues, which requires the diversity philosophy of flexibility. Diversity thinkers know that spending trends of varying ethnic groups and women are examples of areas to be studied for possible organizational marketing opportunities. If this is not considered, businesses may be forced to do the opposite by capitalizing on spending trends and being less flexible by reducing costs.

Effective diversity programs are shown to reduce organizational costs in the long-term, as well as the short-term. Organizations that take a multicultural approach to management and diversity reduce costs associated with high turnover. Diverse groups that are properly managed minimize excessive conflict, which interferes with productivity, communication, and employee morale. Greater morale yields higher productivity and lower time losses. Both are associated with being a net-result of practicing effective diversity thinking.

Again, diversity thinking, when properly employed, incorporates the philosophy that it is always best to promote a talented person of color (or other diversity group) or to include her in some productive way with a development program. As is usually the case, other employees will notice and generally feel more hopeful and committed to the company.

Other Benefits of Diversity

Having a diverse organization yields many other benefits if the programs are well-managed. Productivity is enhanced due to employees building closer relationships to others, because diversity programs promote learning about each employee's unique values, expectations, and goals. Other important ways to increase productivity through diversity include helping others with job objectives, addressing performance issues, and attending to career plans. Job performance, dedication, and attendance are boosted when employees perceive that they are genuinely valued by their organizations. Workplace diversity programs should promote the building of productive relationships, increased career successes, and greater talent pools.

Value can be added to the bottom line of the organization with informal networks, through which many workers can instantly interact with less bureaucracy and less homogeneity from above. Leaders must consciously allow people to be their best by promoting the diversity philosophy that people will always give their best if empowered to do so. This philosophy must be accompanied by leaders helping followers see "what's in it for them."

The Story of the King of Many Kingdoms

In order to illustrate the power of diversity and synergy, I developed the following parable. It involves a king named Orchestro, who was once loved by the people of his kingdom because he was a great listener and was constantly looking for ways to help his people. He was, at that time, considered to be the creator of music since he developed the very first drum. Orchestro had many drums produced by the talented craftsmen of his kingdom, some of which had high tones and some of which sounded very low.

Every year the king would hold a festival of drums. People from all over his kingdom would come to celebrate with the beautiful music heard at the festival of drums.

As a creative leader, King Orchestro encouraged people of his kingdom to create new music. There were contests to see who the best musician was. He also rewarded each talented craftsman with the honor of knighthood when they developed a new drum, contributing to the wonderful music ensembles which were always forming in his kingdom.

After several years of drum festivals, the people of the kingdom were getting bored of the same old thing, and they started to become unhappy and even unruly. The king was also getting bored, and he worried about the unhappy people of his kingdom. He needed to find a way to bring peace back to his kingdom. Of course, annual attendance at the drum festival continued to diminish. After a while, people did not even bother to go at all.

One day, the king decided to assemble a committee of the kingdom's thirty best leaders to find new ways to return excitement and peace to his kingdom. The members were offered rewards for their ideas at the king's round table. The king and his committee decided that it would be best to visit kingdoms all over the world to see what other kings were doing to bring peace and excitement. The king decreed that no member should return home until they found something new to help the kingdom. The loyal members always did what they were told and went away to other lands.

To their own surprise, each quickly found that other kingdoms were having the same problems. Each kingdom was very similar, except none of them had drums. One kingdom had only large brass instruments that played very low tones. The people of this first kingdom also seemed to be looking for a way to cure their boredom and unrest. Although the people of this kingdom spoke a different language, they were friendly.

Also, just like the people of Orchestro's kingdom, they surrounded themselves with people whom they appeared to love and care for.

One of the musicians from the kingdom with the brass instruments was invited to meet King Orchestro and perform. The musician agreed and followed King Orchestro's committee member back to his kingdom. The journey back seemed shorter than Orchestro's follower remembered.

When King Orchestro met the musician, he was amazed by the beauty of the new instrument and loved to hear the wide variety of low tones that came from the horn. The king treated the musician as one of his own, giving him generous gifts and delicious foods.

In another kingdom, Orchestro's second committee member found a man playing what appeared to be a short stick, which was hollowed out and made a high-pitched tone when somebody gently blew through it. There were no drums to be found in this place, and the committee member did not seem to care. All he could think about was the amazingly beautiful and peaceful sound of this new instrument. The second committee member invited the flute musician to meet King Orchestro. The musician agreed and off they went.

In several other kingdoms visited by Orchestro's remaining committee members, musicians were playing instruments that were unique to each of their localities. As the king had requested, each of the remaining committee members invited these musicians to enjoy the hospitality of King Orchestro and his kingdom.

When all of the king's committee members had returned, they realized that they had reached similar findings. The people of each of the other kingdoms spoke different languages, looked, and dressed differently. But, they also found many similarities. All of these musicians had families whom they appeared to love and provide for. They each had an instrument unique to their kingdom—which was the primary entertainment for the people of their respective lands. As in Orchestro's kingdom, the people from each of these kingdoms appeared bored and restless because of the monotony of their lives.

The musicians from each of the far away kingdoms thoroughly enjoyed the hospitality of King Orchestro. With time, they found ways to communicate and build friendships with their fellow musicians and the people of Orchestro's kingdom. Small bands began to form, consisting of three or four musicians. These new bands created beautiful varieties of music that no person of any land had heard before. They found that the more people who were involved in each band, the more beautiful the music was and the happier people seemed to be.

The smaller bands eventually got together to form one large ensemble. More than thirty musicians played together and created songs that all the creatures of the land and air appeared to enjoy. Every man and beast in Orchestro's kingdom found peace and everybody seemed happy through the synergy and power that music created.

The annual drum festival soon became known as the "music festival." King Orchestro invited the people from each of the musicians' homelands to celebrate at the great festival. Wonderful friendships were created and even more people found peace and happiness.

As you may have guessed, the musicians decided to give their ensemble a name, after the generous king who united all of the kingdoms of the earth and brought synergy and peace to the land, calling them themselves an *orchestra*. From that day forward, the kingdoms united and found peace and harmony among themselves. They learned to speak one common language, while keeping their native tongues also in regular communication and to collectively they all learned to show value for the differences between their cultures.

For many years thereafter, there was no war, no boredom, and everybody was made happy through the synergy of music. Decades later, when the king passed away, people never forgot how peace and harmony was created by a wise man that only cared about enriching the lives of others.

CHAPTER FIVE

HOW TO MAKE DIVERSITY PROGRAMS WORK

There are many ways to make diversity programs work. Biases of all types influence the ways that individuals make decisions and act. On a personnel level, all members of the organizations must be reminded to be personally aware of their own culture's values and ways to influence these values through self-awareness. In doing so, it is easier to recognize personal cultural biases through reflections on every individual's past.

After members of the organization analyze their own biases and cultural values, it is easier to build interaction skills through education, case studies, and new knowledge. These in turn will enhance the work environment. Most people will never take the time to think about biases or values, but the greatest personal growth can come by doing so.

When I do diversity workshops, I am always amazed by how many people arrive believing that they know everything there is about diversity. I was quick to learn that this is the first philosophy that needs to be extinguished if I am to do my job at training them to be diversity thinkers.

At my workshops, following my introduction, I pass out a diversity test to help attendees assess how much they know about diversity. On average, most attendees struggle with the test and find that even their best guesses are wrong. Rarely do people get even 60% of the answers correct. Of course, this opens the door for what I have to say and seems to make people pay more attention.

My primary goal for attendees of my workshops is to help them see how to make diversity programs work in their own organizations. I help them to think in terms of diversity philosophies and challenge them to assess their own personal values and biases.

Diversity and Vision Statements

As I discussed above, there are several key areas for you to focus your attention in order to make diversity programs work. Among these key areas is the creation of a vision. The vision must consider where the organization currently is and what you would like it to look like when the vision is realized. The vision must be shared by all the leaders of the organization and must be inculcated into the minds and hearts of everybody involved.

The vision must discuss how diversity will play a part in the overall success of the organization. Details should be written in a company vision statement or some document for members to regularly review. A new vision statement may entail creating or altering an existing vision statement. It should include a definition of diversity that works specifically for the organization. I recommend that the definition of diversity found in vision statements be broad enough for no employee to feel excluded. And of course, the vision must be communicated to all employees in order for it to work.

Assessment and Organizational Diversity Success

Another crucial component of making diversity programs work is conducting audits, which includes finding out how each employee feels about corporate diversity efforts to determine important issues that need to be addressed. This step should also include reviewing and measuring the success of Equal Employment Opportunity (EEO) plans. Leaders must also not forget to review policies, procedures, and to examine employee exit interviews—looking for possible common reasons leading to the current turnover rate of the organization.

After audits have been conducted, senior managers should discuss proposals for plans of change that pertain to diversity. It is important to keep managers engaged and involved with the process of making any formal diversity plans so that they will understand how they work. In addition, a side benefit is to spark motivation to take further necessary steps of implementing the plan.

Once the diversity plan is implemented, another assessment process should be instigated to evaluate what is working well and what needs to be corrected. When this occurs, information from the initial audit should be used to rewrite, edit, and delete any rules, policies, and practices that appear biased, unfair or discriminatory toward any group. Any systems that impede the progress of diversity measures should also be considered for revision during this time.

Training organizational members is the next area of focus in implementing diversity programs. This may be difficult because organizational change is often resisted by a majority, as discussed in previous chapters. As I have suggested earlier, effective communication is the key to buy-in. Communicating and showing each individual he can personally benefit by supporting the diversity change is crucial. This will enhance support and confidence, which will be needed for the proper implementation of change. In turn, this will eventually benefit the organization as a whole.

Finally, a reassessment process must take place. Leaders should establish a diversity task force comprised of a cross-sectional representative of the organization. The members of this task force should include people who are well-respected at every level of the organization. If human resources are involved, there should be limited reporting to HR members. Diversity programs must not be seen as *"just another HR program"*. It must be seen as a plan put together for the people, by the people.

Input from all members of organizational teams should be invited, accepted, and considered during every meeting. Communication is not productive unless every person has an opportunity to share her ideas and observations. When all members have concluded that the necessary measures have been successfully implemented and are working smoothly, the task force members have done their job to ensure that the diversity program is on the right track. Diversity task force members should then double-check that things are closely aligned with the organizational vision statement. When this is completed, the task force members can distribute assignments to set the necessary changes in motion and schedule a follow-up meeting.

Measuring Diversity Success and Training

One way to implement change, as mentioned in previous chapters, is with the use of benchmarking. Benchmarking should outline specific obtainable goals. Communication to all leading members of the organization about the specific goals should be made regularly. All levels of the organization must be included in any training and communication so that progress can be made uniformly. Performance must be monitored, continually evaluated, and revised as necessary.

In alignment with diversity thinking, effective communication throughout the organization is essential in order to yield the benefits of a diverse workplace. Special measures must be implemented, if not already in place to distribute the information effectively. Email, memos, video conferences, and newsletters are only a few of the best ways to get a message across.

Training and education should also be considered key aspects of the communication process. Training can help make diversity visible in all aspects of the organization and help organizational members to work better with diversity.

Steps for Creating a Diversity Program

How to begin: First, identify the diversity groups that are not represented in management and in diversity planning teams. Find out why. Sometimes the answer is that no one qualified is available to fill the position. If this is the answer, rest assured that things may be going well and no changes may need to take place.

Human resource managers know how expensive complaints about improper diversity measures can be. It is therefore important to create diverse teams that are given the proper resources to be productive and happy.

Take a look at the demographics of your customers. Are they adequately represented in your workforce? If not, your organization may be missing out on opportunities to completely satisfy their wants and needs. If this is the case, you may be losing customers and revenues to someone who better exhibits diversity.

Summing Up How to Make it Work

Conclusively, studies show that diversity is still not visible at all times in every organization. Therefore, processes must be considered in order to effectively manage diversity strategies and make it consistently visible. Diversity strategies must be properly evaluated and implemented. To implement an effective diversity program, the organization's cultural environment (along with management and their evaluation systems) should be examined to ascertain if existing personnel and human resource processes will support or hinder diversity within the organization. Once this assessment is done, a strategic plan can be put into action.

Putting a plan into action requires strategic alignment and proper management by organizational leaders. Diversity must be managed at three levels simultaneously: Individual, interpersonal, and organizational.

Teaching members of organizations to value the differences between individuals is the first component of educating and changing the organization. Changing attitudes about how people are different and fostering the acceptance of individual differences should be the common goal of diversity programs.

Diversity programs should also focus on how people are similar and help members evaluate personal values and biases that they may have in order to see them as reflections of our value systems that affect the way we act.

Diversity training should promote the organizational outcome of diverse perspectives leading to creative ideas and innovative processes. *The diversity philosophy of synergy* states that the outcome of few working together bringing unique talents ideas and yields more together than individuals working on their own.

The bottom-line: Managing diversity involves changing the mindsets of both managers and employees. This takes a shift of thinking and assumptions. It involves evaluating biases and values, and must incorporate continued and ongoing diversity education.

People must be shown that change is necessary in a positive way and always for the benefit of the success. People must learn to value and respect every person and reflect upon similarities as well as differences.

As a result of a properly implemented diversity program, the organization will be more creative, competitive, productive and healthy. Everybody wins!

CHAPTER SIX

COMMON MISTAKES OF DIVERSITY PROGRAMS

Diversity programs have been implemented in numerous organizations over the past three decades. As a result, books and articles filled with people's experiences and philosophies on what works and what doesn't abound. This book was inspired in part by those writings and also with my own experiences as a consultant. There are several common mistakes that everyone should know, so that they can avoid falling into a common trap. Please consider some of the following ideas as you manage diversity in your life and organization.

Mistake # 1: Not Just a Race Issue

First of all, diversity should not just be thought of as just a race issue. If a company wants to maximize the benefits that diversity can bring, it must understand who is involved when diversity is being considered. By now, the word diversity should be well understood along the following lines: **Valuing and utilizing the unique talents, ideas, and contributions of people of differing backgrounds.** Moreover, diversity is a reflection of "otherness," or the personal qualities that differ from one's own self. These backgrounds include race, but also goes beyond ethnic lines. When most people hear the word "diversity," they think of someone's racial background as it pertains to country of origin or culture. However, diversity also refers to, age, gender, physical ability, sexual orientation, religion, language, and other differences people may have. It can also refer to background differences in social class, profession, culture, skills, and values.

Thorough diversity training programs should discuss communication and interaction with each of those groups. Failure to do so undermines the potential effectiveness of diversity programs. In addition, just because a certain group is not represented doesn't mean that diversity should be ignored in that regard, because someday, an individual from that group might join the organization.

Mistake #2: Celebrating Diversity Takes Care of Everything

Some organizations also appear to think that because they celebrate diversity, they are taking the correct measures in *utilizing* diversity. Diversity celebrations, such as ethnic potlucks and parties with ethnic themes allow people with different backgrounds to better understand those cultures. Celebrating definitely has its place. However, it cannot be the primary method of taking action.

An actual training program is necessary because strong internal biases must be addressed.

Personal values need to be considered by each individual, and soul searching must take place. Formalized training and education helps to do that, and reading books on diversity help a great deal too. Diversity programs must be evaluated, implemented, trained, and reevaluated, as discussed in prior chapters. Teaching best-practices for managing diversity must be engrained in the mission and vision statements of the organization.

Diversity programs must actively look for ways to involve people of every available background in crucial decision-making processes and leadership roles. Diversity should be considered a crucial business issue that needs to be addressed at all times for the benefit of the organization as a whole. Likewise, diversity programs are the responsibility of everyone in the company, not just Human Resources. Every person who holds a formal leadership title needs to be involved. Leaders must be encouraged to endorse diversity-thinking in every component of their decision-making processes. All members of the organization need to understand how important diversity thinking is to the organization's success.

Mistake #3: Recruiting is the Primary Program

A third common mistake of organizational leaders is that diversity programs are limited to recruitment policies. Diversity programs are much more than recruiting and hiring challenges. They should be recognized as internal opportunities, as well. Training is the key, and promoting internal candidates is crucial. The best way to improve employee morale is to promote from within. As I have mentioned throughout this book, promoting qualified people of non-traditional backgrounds to positions of responsibility stimulates employee morale. Happy employees are productive ones.

Mistake #4: Tokenism

Tokenism can be a problem for organizations implementing diversity programs. Putting select people in certain roles because of their backgrounds creates a valid perception of tokenism. Every person hired or promoted to do a job should be qualified and should be clearly the best person for the job.

When people spread rumors that people have been promoted primarily because of background and not qualifications, organizations must address the gossip immediately. Leaders should explicitly state that only the most qualified people will fill job vacancies. Deviating from this practice for the sake of pleasing diversity programs can be costly in many ways. For example, promoting unqualified colleagues because of background and not qualifications undermines the systems of the organization. People may lose confidence and believe that decision makers are not capable of making the best decisions for the company. When this philosophy is adopted by onlookers, they begin to question any and all other decisions from that individual.

An obvious outcome of employing tokenism and promoting someone who is not the most qualified is clearly depicted when the duties of the job will not get done as efficiently as they would be if someone more qualified had been chosen. All sorts of further issues are associated with this scenario. Resentment could cause rifts in the cohesiveness of work teams. Other related jobs and systems that depend on the unqualified person may suffer, and breakdowns in productivity and effectiveness will occur.

Mistake #5: Shifts in Organizational Dynamics

Sometimes when organizations implement diversity programs, organizational power dynamics shift. One group may weigh heavily over other groups in representation and cause rifts in teams. People who once felt appreciated may feel that they are devalued due to leadership changes. Opinions may also become less heard and used. People of certain backgrounds may get fewer opportunities to participate when others are getting more than their share.

The Solutions in Diversity Training

Organizational diversity training sessions should welcome participants to share stories that deal with each of the challenges mentioned above. Intent behind the discussions should be analyzed for ways to avoid common mistakes and overcome challenges in order to make diversity programs work. Group members in training sessions should be asked helpful questions and given ideas to ponder, including the analysis of the organization's current place on an "intolerance-appreciation continuum." Discussions of how implementation should occur and how to monitor evaluation of organizational operations should be conducted and encouraged.

Other possible thoughts for discussion among members of the organization might include examining the processes for selecting leaders. Members should evaluate current informal methods of choosing teams, promotions, and organizational education. Discussions and thoughts about job satisfaction, promotion, teams, and progress may assist in diversity training.

These are only a few examples of training questions. The list of questions is endless. The purpose of diversity training is to get people to understand the value of diversity and that every member should be considered a valuable contributor to the organization's success. Training sessions help people become satisfied with their jobs. In turn, they are likely to be more pleasant to their coworkers and bosses and are less likely to quit than those who are dissatisfied.

By now, you have read the majority of the book. Ask yourself the following questions and evaluate how happy you are with your answers.

What is your definition of diversity? How many diversity groups can you name? Why is it important to include all differing backgrounds in your list of diversity groups? What specific areas of your organization should consider diversity training? What should be the primary factors in hiring and promoting as it relates to diversity thinking? Why is celebrating diversity important to your organization? How can celebrating diversity be a problem for you?

The answers to those questions most-likely will tell you a little bit about yourself. What are they saying about your organization? What are your areas of opportunity? Where does your organization need to go from here?

CHAPTER SEVEN

ANALYZING THE SUCCESS OF ORGANIZATIONAL DIVERSITY

So you have done your part in making sure that diversity programs have been properly installed in your organization. People seem to be happy. There are signs of diversity thinking everywhere you turn. Well, how do you know that everything is going according to plan? The truth is that most organizations don't realize there is a problem until it's gone from bad to worse.

By this point in the book, you know that diversity is important. But the fact of the matter is that most people are far more focused on what needs to get done in their everyday work. Very few people have the privilege of making diversity thinking their priority.

Sure, the occasional diversity training and diversity task force meeting are required attendance, but diversity thinking is generally done when we have a scheduled opportunity to incorporate it into lives. That said, what can we do to make sure that diversity programs are successful? The answer is simple. Organizations need to be *proactive* and employ a few straightforward steps.

Step number one. Take a look around. Who has been with the company since the diversity initiative was first implemented? Who is new to the company?

Step number two. If there are people no longer are working for the company, find out why they left, and, if possible, find out where they went. If they are no longer with the company, chances are they will be open and honest about why they left. Many companies use exit interviews when an employee quits. Ideally, information gleaned from these exit interviews is used to improve conditions within the company and to assess if others are doing what they are supposed to be doing.

Additionally, if employee turnover rates for female and minority managers are higher than those of Caucasian-male managers, there may be a problem. Find out the reasons for this being the case. Perhaps no job openings have been available since the diversity program has been installed. Or better yet, perhaps everybody is doing an excellent job and is completely satisfied with their current work situations.

Step number three. Conduct your own research. Take a look at the managers and people holding leadership roles. What diversity groups do they represent? How qualified are these leaders? How long have they held their positions? How successful have they been with accomplishing company goals? How do their followers feel about them? Are they well-respected by others in the company?

The answers to these questions are common sense. Create a tally sheet of your organization and see for yourself if your diversity program is working the way that it should. If not, find a way to get the information into the right hands to make the necessary changes.

If employers don't place both female and other diversity group candidates into management jobs, there may be a problem. Ideally, women and minorities who report directly to senior managers should receive promotions to senior-level jobs at equal rates to White men. This creates balance and harmony. Importantly, onlookers will believe the organization treats people fairly—much more than people who see only Caucasian males running everything. For these reasons, among others, women and other diversity groups should share equally in job assignments that increase learning and enhance career opportunities. Organizations that make this adjustment will find better ways to do things and will thrive in the ways discussed earlier in this book.

Step number four. Ask employees at every level of the organization to explain the company's stance on diversity. Chances are that you will find employees who don't know the answer to that question. You may find that they have no idea of what the company's vision statement is. Worse yet, some may not even see how what they do contributes to the overall success of the company.

Diversity thinking needs to be much more than a company program. It must be a living, active part of the organization's culture. It must live in every employee in some profound way.

When you analyze the answers to my questions, you may find that nothing needs to be done. If this is the case, congratulate yourself and those responsible for making it happen. Celebrate it with others.

Do not forget to implement your diversity evaluation on a semi-annual basis. If you do not have the time to do so, make sure that you hire a qualified professional to do an assessment of your organization. It will be worth the cost in the long run.

If you find that changes need to be made, be proactive in taking the necessary steps. Remember that companies that promote proper diversity thinking are generally more productive and profitable than those who do not.

Chapter Review

Review the following questions and see how you feel about the answers you give about each. Be proactive to make any changes you deem necessary. Evaluate your responses as it fits into your own value system. Are you the person who you wish to be? How is your organization doing?

On what occasions do most leaders in your company discuss diversity? What steps do you think would best analyze diversity success in your organization? What can you do to minimize the number of personnel who leave your company dissatisfied? What specific areas of diversity should be equally filled by women and members of other diversity groups in your organization? What should be done when a diversity program confirms success? Who should you contact to ensure that diversity is properly working to maximize the efficiency and productivity of your organization?

CHAPTER EIGHT

CREATING CHANGE IN ORGANIZATIONAL TEAMS AND SYSTEMS

Contemporary scholarly literature suggests that people who are carefully trained to work together in teams tend to be happier and more productive than those who are simply thrown together without any definite organizational support. This means that leaders should make sure that two or more people are assigned to accomplish company tasks and organizational goals whenever possible.

When evaluating teams for success, it is necessary to analyze how each diversity issue is being managed in order to maximize the organization's productivity. Doing so may show that changes may need to be made. A few reasons that change may need to be made are directly tied to diversity thinking. Change may be crucial for the sake of fixing or maximizing communication. Perhaps some teams have members who speak multiple languages, but are only proficient in one. If this is the case, including someone else on the team who can speak that language and also the predominant language of the organization is best.

Communication Challenges

Communication is not only about a formal language, such as Chinese, French, or Spanish; it may also be about culture. People of one generation may not completely understand the actions and intentions behind the statements of others outside of their generation. Some terms may have different connotations than were intended by the sender of the message. Pairing people who can relate to each other or who are sensitive to other cultures may be the key to maximizing teams with these communication characteristics.

Diversity and Social Responsibility

Disadvantaged social groups often benefit from employing diversity thinking, which means their communities benefit, too. By diversifying workforces, individuals can break out from patterns of inopportunity and earn a living, achieving their dreams. Employing diversity thinking in hiring and promoting also has an economic payback. Think about how it may be affecting the workers' communities by alleviating the local economic tax structures. By diversifying the workforce, people are effectively transformed from tax users into tax payers.

Diversity for Legal Reasons

Organizations that employ diversity thinking and programs also benefit for legal reasons. Teams that are intentionally infused with diversity change the way business is done. Legal terms include non-discriminatory employment practices legislation,

non-compliance with Equal Employment
Opportunity, or Affirmative Action legislation.
Every day, people sue employers for alleged
discriminatory practices. Fines and lawsuits can
become very expensive for businesses that do not
practice effective workforce diversification.

From a legal perspective, it does not make sense
to refuse to hire and promote qualified people of
multicultural and differing backgrounds. Fair
business practice, when steadily enforced, cannot
be easily dismissed as evidence when faced with
lawsuits or fines.

Teams comprised of people representing
diversity help organizations better market their
products and services and give unique niches
for marketing. From a marketing perspective,
buying power is represented by people of all
ethnicities, gender, and sexual orientations.
To ensure products and services are being
designed to appeal to the greatest customer
base, intelligent companies should hire with
diversity practices in mind, in order to better
understand the needs of the customers with
similar backgrounds. Organizations truly do
benefit when workforces mirror the customer
base of the organization.

Warning for Diversity Thinkers

Although people of similar backgrounds may have many things in common, including food, entertainment, and language (to name a few), effective diversity thinkers should remember that *no two people are identical.* If you know what one Cambodian person likes, another Cambodian will not necessarily like the same things. Chances are that that person may be completely different, so do not fall into the common trap of stereotyping.

Finally . . .

When organizations practice effective diversity measures, business communication strategies are enhanced. Numerous companies are seeing a diverse workforce growing around them in vendors, partners, and customers. When the employee bases match the people they interact with—the organization's customers, vendors, and related companies—the organization can communicate more effectively and improve creativity and production.

Problem solving is maximized when diversity thinking is employed. Companies can adapt to new situations, readily identify new opportunities, and quickly capitalize on them. Capacity can be measured by the range of talent experience, knowledge, insight, and imagination available in the workforce.

Properly implementing diversity thinking is best characterized by companies that find new successes by valuing employees for unique qualities and perspectives. These companies are both small and large. See if you can pick which ones they are. Is yours one of them?

Chapter Review

Answer the following questions. After reading this chapter, think about how you define a team. What does "team" mean to you? Why are teams more effective than individuals? What side benefits might diversity thinking provide for your organization? What legal benefits can diversity thinking provide for your company? What stereotypes do you personally hold, but know are not necessarily true? How could your organization benefit from diversity? If you had the power to influence change (and you do), what would you suggest to the decision-makers of your organization?

CHAPTER NINE

A PLAN FOR ORGANIZATIONAL DIVERSITY

Although organizations differ in size, demographics, culture, products and services offered, they have one thing in common—people. As many contemporary writers attest, there are "natural laws" that people must follow in order to be effective. Whether or not one wants to believe in natural laws, one cannot deny that they just seem to exist and work. Failing to abide by them often causes people to be less effective and generally unhappy.

Many natural laws deal with a need to act and be treated with *honesty*. No person wants to be deceived, and no conscientious person feels good when they lie or know they are hearing lies. Integrity is the most agreed upon leadership attribute addressed in academic and business literature that identify leadership traits. It is therefore prudent for leaders to be honest in every matter. Failing to do so will deteriorate their credibility and power.

Truly great leaders will openly admit when they lack knowledge or make a mistake, and they will apologize for any damage it may have caused. They also actively do their best to right the wrongs they have caused—no matter the financial cost. For instance, the leaders at Tylenol recently recognized that their pain-relief capsules and packaging could be easily tampered with. People actually died, not because of the direct negligence of the manufacturer, but by the harmful tampering of others with bad intentions. Out of integrity and exemplary leadership, the makers of Tylenol lost millions of dollars by recalling all existing capsules from of the shelves of retailers. This act of integrity saved the name of the manufacturer, and today is still recognized as a dependable company that can be trusted by both doctors and families.

On the other hand, the notorious leaders at Enron, an extinct American power distribution company, were dishonest and corrupt. Court proceedings found the leaders to be less than honest about accounting procedures and financials when discussed with their employees and consumers. The company went bankrupt because of their poor business decisions, illegal doctoring of accounts, and their dishonesty.

When the systems and actions of organizational leaders focus on integrity, diversity programs prosper. Every employee must feel that they are being treated with integrity and be given the opportunity to act with integrity. Whether or not you follow the Bible, one cannot deny the universal truths and wisdom of the Hebrew scriptures of the Old Testament expression that "Truth begets truth." Honest dealings with people generate trust, and trust will open new levels of friendship and future opportunities for interaction.

The opposite is also true. When most people feel that they have been deceived, they will not trust that individual or organization so openly. Employees will not be so willing to give their best, and coworkers will feel less secure with their company.

In addition to honesty, the natural law of *listening* must also be considered. People must be heard fully heard *first* in order for communication to be successful. The most effective leaders in history were successful when they truly heard the needs of their constituents and showed that they could deliver. For example, in 2006, Democrats showed their strong opposition to the war in Iraq. In Connecticut, the incumbent Joseph Lieberman, an 18-year senator and former vice-presidential candidate, lost the Democratic primary because of his support for the war. Political experts believe that if Lieberman had listened to his constituents and took a solid stance against the war, he could have won that primary race. His adherence to other natural laws helped him win the November election as an independent.

Another natural law, the law of *progression and change,* includes several useful themes. The first and most dominant is that nothing ever stays the same. People, nature, and systems are always evolving, so we must learn to adapt. The best leaders are both flexible and constantly doing things to actively grow. Two of my favorite books on change, authored by Dr. Michael Beitler, suggest that change is the only thing in the universe that is ever constant. When putting an organizational diversity plan of action together, there must be systems in place that evaluate how to deal with change—both initializing and managing it.

Putting Your Diversity Plan Together

An important aspect to consider is a step-by-step plan to take advantage of diversity. The question, "Why are you doing this?" must be asked in order to recognize the need for diversity. It provokes further questions about what is happening in the organization, the local community, or the customer base.

I recommend researching a starting point and identifying internal areas for concern. This is done by asking the people in the organization about what is going on. Organizational culture must be assessed. What are the likes, dislikes, and current needs of the members of the organization and its customers? Why do current employees enjoy working for the organization? Why do current customers keep coming back? What aspects of the organization's culture are desirable to these two groups?

When these questions are assessed through questionnaires, they should be integrated into the diversity program, and all major decision makers should be made aware of the findings of an organizational cultural audit. They must learn to support these findings and be encouraged to find ways to incorporate these understandings into their leadership style.

Education is a central component of putting a diversity plan into action. Recent studies show that people who know their own personal cultural history and understand their own cultural distinctions are more effective than people who do not. Similarly, organizational members must become familiar with the organization's history and culture. In order to take the organization to the next level, progressive education must take place. Such learning can come in many forms. The easiest way is through company newsletters and email. Articles can be written to help all organizational members know the major accomplishments of the company. People in the organization must see how the company has changed for the better over the years in order to maintain levels of competitiveness.

Members must see that change is necessary and acknowledge the usefulness of certain practices of the organization, while at the same time recognizing that what was once useful to the organization may not still be beneficial and therefore must be changed. Employees need to be given the choice to accept cultural changes and be shown through education why changes are necessary.

Employees must learn about what appeals most to their colleagues and the customers and why it is important to preserve these aspects within the culture and make changes in their personal routines and beliefs to support the organization's culture. Every employee must see that they each play a crucial role in supporting the organization. Likewise, they must see that their non-support can have a derogatory effect on the success of the competitiveness of the organization.

In summary, I suggest that organizations ask their clients and employees about the most appealing aspects of the organization's culture. Communication with people in leadership positions is an important aspect in this plan.

It should be made clear to all employees that diversity programs benefit the company.

It is important to achieve buy-in and understanding on the part of the company leaders and as many of the key employees as possible. The secret to this is engaging and involving as many people in the process as possible. Getting buy-in also depends on keeping the training interesting and fun. Newsletters, email, and company web sites may be crucial tools for disseminating diversity training and related historical and cultural information.

The next section focuses further on the educational aspect of diversity programs, which is the most important aspect of an effective diversity program. Without education, people will not see a reason to change. The organization cannot create successful change unless leaders and followers understand why it must occur and how crucial their personal support of the changes is.

Hot Washing

The US military uses a technique that they call "hot washing." This common practice is conducted by leaders and constituents after simulations and drills. It involves a formal meeting of the participants and leaders to document what went right and find ways to troubleshoot how to fix what went wrong.

So too it should be with organizations implementing diversity programs. Change is best managed when decision makers involve the active participation of the people who are affected and involved. This includes employees of all levels of the organization, customers, outside suppliers and organizational leaders.

Ideally, these formalized change meetings must be structured so that people will feel like they truly have an active role in making a difference. They must not be treated as inferiors, according to the chain of command or organizational hierarchy. They must be treated as valuable individuals with equal voices in creating change.

The change environment must be free enough where people can speak their mind without fear of repercussion. Trust must be supported and encouraged to flourish by every person involved. Words must be positive throughout the change meetings. The processes must be documented and plans for follow-up and action must be drafted. Participants must know what is expected from them when they leave the meeting and reasonable benchmarks must be outlined to give a roadmap to success.

Organizational change should have processes that adhere to minimum legal standards. Checking for success and monitoring should be done as an ongoing process. Celebrating the program along the way should also occur. Celebration can be done in many different ways. The creative aspects of celebrating could and should be left to everyone who is interested in making it happen. Special funding and time should be allocated to such celebrations. Whether the celebration comes as a lunch time buffet or a weekend get-together; a venue and time should be chosen so that most people can benefit and participate. It will be most effective when more people are involved in the planning process.

Chapter Review

Please consider the following questions. What is common among all organizations that might help your company? Which natural laws might come into play in your successful diversity program? What is the most desirable trait of a leader in your organization? What steps should be taken toward putting together a diversity program for your organization? What is the most important component of making a diversity program work in your environment? How could hot washing be used in your organization? What could celebrating diversity program successes look like in your organization?

CHAPTER TEN

DIVERSITY TRAINING PROCESS

Some of the most eye-opening experiences can come during diversity training. Formalized diversity workshops are the only way that people can fully understand the benefits of diversity and do the powerful work of personal evaluation, which is needed to accomplish diversity success. As you read this chapter, imagine yourself as a participant of the workshop I describe.

In order to get the most out of a diversity training session four steps must be taken. **The first step** involves understanding your own culture.

- What is your own culture?
- What particular elements make it distinct?
- What elements are similar to other cultures?
- What kind of impact does your cultural background have on the way you see the world and act?

Remember, your reality is your own and nobody else's. The way you were raised and your cultural underpinnings affect what you believe to be real. Your paradigm is what you believe is true in every situation. A paradigm shift may be needed in order to benefit others, your organization, or yourself.

The second step of diversity training is to see how culture impacts your organization, social groups, and the world around you. Can you identify what distinct cultural beliefs and influences are at work where you work?

The third step of diversity training is perhaps the most difficult. It involves recognizing your own biases.

- What stereotypes do you carry?
- What assumptions and prejudgments do you practice?
- In which ways do you discriminate?

It is human to have stereotypes and prejudgments. Everyone has prejudices. As humans, we learn through a process of experiencing something and assuming that similar situations will reoccur. Experiential learning is very powerful and cannot be avoided.

Judgments are created; and biases and assumptions are formed. The most effective people are aware of those prejudgments and biases; and actively take those in to consideration before acting.

The final step of diversity training involves learning about other cultures and building interaction skills. Sometimes problems occurring at work stem from misunderstandings due to cultural differences. Learning about the differences between your coworkers and how to best interact with them takes proactive initiative, inquiry, and training.

Training may involve reading books on diversity, evaluating case studies, interactive roll-plays, videos, and discussion. Training must be done in a way that maintains the interests of everyone involved. People learn in different ways, which is discussed later in this chapter.

I am always amazed that at every diversity workshop how so many people appear to feel they understand diversity fully. Many people come to diversity workshops because they are required by their organizations to attend and do not fully want to be there. I can remember feeling the same way at one I attended, but did not host.

Winning with Diversity Workshops

I challenge participants in my classes and workshops to make every encounter a learning experience and to deeply challenge what they already believe and be open to growing with new ideas. With that said, I begin my workshops with a diversity quiz that asks questions to assist in showing participants what they know and don't know about differing cultures. Sample questions from this quiz are included in the back of this book. If you would like to take the entire quiz, contact me via email: *dr.paul@paulgerhardt.com*.

After workshop participants take the diversity test, we score it together. Participants are asked to be honest about how accurate they were in answering the questions. I also encourage participants to share more about what they know in relation to the questions as we continue correcting their quizzes. The quiz serves as an eye-opener and sets a tone of openness for learning. Rarely will a group score even 50% of the questions right. People often share with me after their training sessions that the diversity quiz was a powerful learning tool.

All workshops work best when people get to know each other better and personal barriers are broken down. My students learn more about me as their instructor and gain confidence in my experiences and knowledge, as well as know that I am there to genuinely help them in any way that I can. I encourage students/participants to get to know their workshop peers in the same way through an introductory ice-breaker.

Ice-Breaker

My favorite ice-breaker is a treasure hunt for personal commonalities and dissimilarities. Participants are given a time limit, dependent upon how many participants are present. I allow enough time for learners to talk to as many participants as possible. In this allotted time, they must them share one commonality and difference about themselves from a list I distribute.

Once they have used half the allocated time for creating their lists, I request that they find one person from the other side of the room. They must not know that person and are required to gather a short story about one of the topics from the list that is not common with the other person. At the conclusion of the time allocated for collecting the information, I ask participants to return to their seats and discuss the stories they heard. I also ask participants to reflect on the benefits of the project. I hope that people discover that regardless of age or background, that people still have many things in common.

Of course another benefit is that people's differences have benefits to others in terms of experience and knowledge. At the same time, people at the workshop will be better able to open up and participate more freely in the learning session.

Expected Learning Outcomes

My workshops are created to be informative and enjoyable for all. I open the communication lines by sharing with participants what the expected learning outcomes will be. I encourage everybody to participate freely and often, as well as ask questions—knowing that no question is ever stupid.

My workshops are customized to meet the needs of each individual organization that hires me. Common expected learning outcomes include:

- Developing a better understanding of different cultures' norms and values.
- Receiving valuable tips on communicating with others.
- Avoiding misunderstandings.
- Evaluating personal biases.
- Building effective relationships.
- Understanding diversity-thinking and terminology.

After discussing the intended outcomes, I often open the floor to questions for clarifying expected outcomes and request that others share their interests of further information they would like to learn. If the requests are expected to go beyond the scope of the workshop or will take up more time than is allotted, I will do my best to answer their questions. I always leave my contact information with participants so that I might answer any further questions they might have. As a read of my book, I welcome you to do the same.

Ground Rules

The next portion of my workshops usually includes putting together some agreed upon ground rules. In this section of the training I invite all participants to share at least one idea each—that they feel will help create a learning environment that maximizes the benefits of such a meeting. As participants share their ideas, I write them down and help clarify each one as they are shared. I encourage learners to include rules that encourage respect and trust among peers. I always ask that one rule include anonymity and discretion, so that personal information or stories that are shared will be kept in the room and not shared with others who might misinterpret it or harm the participants' reputations.

Impact of Culture on Work

In order for diversity training to be effective, participants at my workshops are then shown how a rich culture positively impacts organizations. The more a person understands how much influence culture has on an organization, the more effective communication can be among members.

Specifically, effective diversity training sessions focus on evaluating both personal and organizational values and beliefs that directly affect the behaviors of its members. In turn, diversity programs help people develop behaviors that will help them manage diversity and demonstrate the value that diversity brings.

To learn how to value and manage diversity, people must learn how to actively change their behaviors, but not all of their values. Values are the most difficult thing for a person to change because they have been rooted in childhood and shaped over a lifetime. Most values are good and do not need to be changed. People with truly

open minds will know what to do and when
to do it after attending an effective workshop.

Communication Role-Play

In order to keep the workshops educational and
entertaining, there must be constant interaction
between the facilitator and the audience. Equally
important is having the participants interact with
each other, to share their ideas, experiences, and
talents.

One of the most powerful ways of teaching how
people with different backgrounds communicate is
done through a controlled role-play. My favorite
communication role-play involves the participation
of four to eight participants from the audience,
who I "screen" and select by watching their real
communication styles during our interactions of
the day. If I have noticed the participant is quiet,
I secretly give him the role of communicating
loudly. If a participant uses her hands excessively
when she speaks, I secretly ask her to keep her
hands behind her back when talking. If another
seems like he requires a large bubble of personal
space, I ask him to stand very close to his partner
and invade his personal space.

These secret roles are passed out on small slips of paper with the accompanying task of communicating with an assigned partner who does not know what the other person's role is. As you may have imagined, it is very interesting to see the partners communicating with each other. I usually ask one pair of partners to perform their role-plays in front of the larger group with the larger group quietly assessing whatever they can about each demonstration in a following wrap-up session.

The outcome of such a communication exercise is powerful when experienced firsthand. The bottom-line of this project is to show that every person communicates in his own way. Communication is most effective when we can do it in a way that will be best-received by each individual.

Although your communication style may work best for you, it is much more powerful to understand how others best receive information, which is often in the same manner in which they communicate. Look for clues about how people receive information best. If a person uses statements like, "I see." Chances are that that person is a visual communicator. To communicate best with such a person, paint pictures of what you are saying with words using visual descriptors and lots of adjectives.

When people use there hands a lot while speaking, they most-likely are kinesthetic learners. Help that type of person understand through communication that involves hands-on learning or descriptive language that is experiential in nature.

It is also beneficial to know that numerous psychological studies show that communicators who mirror the actions and speech patterns of others will be better received and liked. However, mirroring should not be done in an obvious way.

Understanding Why Diversity is Important

After a short break in the first portion of my diversity workshops, I start the next segment with a short story describing why diversity is important. I talk about how organizations must understand and be understanding of individual clients and employees' cultural backgrounds. Culture is learned and is not innate. Exact culture is not always shared by all persons with similar backgrounds, but some aspects will be shared and will definitely have an impact on the ways they believe and must be treated.

For example, some American companies may make the mistake of assuming that the British are exactly like Americans. What many do not account for, even though they speak a very similar language, is that British culture has a different class system. The expectations that accompany such an underlying class system are deeply engrained in the culture and could cause deep misunderstandings if not observed. Having people who understand these differences can help enhance those particular relationships. Thus, by considering these differences, a company will be more effective than a competitor that might not have such an understanding.

As I have stated before, no two people are the same. We cannot assume that just because one person believed a certain way that another person who may look similar to that person will feel the same. I recommend finding a tactful way of asking if saying or doing things that were expected by others would be OK. If done in a way that conveys personal respect for the other, it will usually be thankfully received. It is better to build relationships with others that our founded on trust and appreciation.

Trust can be best built by learning as much as you can about people's backgrounds, likes, and dislikes. Effective leaders should keep an open mind and encourage others to do the same. It is also very important, as I discuss further, for diversity thinkers to become familiar with their own personal prejudices and stereotypes. Knowing what they are can be very powerful in taking the next steps to make the most out of every relationship.

The most effective educational sessions I facilitate occur when participants share their experiences and knowledge with each other about working with someone of a differing culture. Also, in most of my workshops I ask participants to discuss their experiences and ideas openly as to how best work with others of differing backgrounds and learn what they think works best.

In one segment of my workshop, we sometimes discuss the benefits for well-managed diversity. I openly invite all participants to share what benefits they each think diversity has at work. I usually get some great responses that make participants think—myself included.

Many of the rationale has already been expressed earlier in this book. During workshops, I have found that it is helpful to write them down for everyone to see. How many can you come up with on your own?

One story to illustrate how understanding diversity can have a powerful impact on how we do business comes from a real experience that was shared to me by a friend. This story has numerous variations in life. Have you heard one similar to it? Bill (a pseudonym) worked at a meat cutter for over thirty years. He was African-American, divorced, and very tight with his money. After saving for many years, Bill was getting ready for retirement. He owned his home free and clear. He promised himself when he retired that he would reward himself by buying a brand new Lincoln Continental.

At age 60, on a beautiful Saturday summer evening after getting off of work; Bill drove to the local Lincoln dealership. He walked into the showroom ready to buy the car of his dreams. He was dressed in his work clothes. They were neither rags nor were they new. Bill was a proud man, but still a very frugal one.

Bill approached the first salesman's desk, who initially ignored him. Then he spoke louder stating that he wanted to go for a test ride in his favorite model of Lincoln in the sales parking lot. The salesman rudely looked up at Bill and told him that he was sure that it would be a waste of his time. "Company policy stated that they could not show cars to people who they felt could not afford to purchase the vehicle." Bill quickly turned around without saying a word back to the salesman and drove home without his dream car. Bill had a bitter taste in his mouth and could not get that experience out of his mind.

On his way home, Bill could not help but think about his dream car and how much he resented being slighted by the salesman. He went to church the next morning, where he was a well-respected deacon. After services, Bill drove back to the dealership in his best Sunday suit. He walked directly past the salesman who snubbed him the previous day. He talked to a woman who worked there, and she let him drive the car. It was a quick sale.

After completing the deal with this salesperson, Bill proudly walked up to the desk of the man from the day before and smugly told him, "I purchased ALL of the extras and paid cash on the full sticker. It is the finest Lincoln on the lot!" Bill smiled as he drove away from the dealership in his dream car.

After hearing my friend's story, I thought of how much of a commission that the first salesperson must have lost because of his own prejudgments. Has an experience like this ever happened to you?

Understanding the Way People Learn

Effective leaders, teachers, and seminar leaders know that people learn through a variety of ways. As I mentioned before, when people make a comment like, "I see." Chances are that that person is a visual learner. This means that if you want to communicate best with that person, find a way to paint a picture with words.

People who make statements like, "I can hear what you are saying" are likely auditory learners. Communication will be most effective with these learners when it is spoken.

People also learn through a hands-on approach. This kinesthetic style of learning may involve exercises where the participants practice doing what they are meant to learn. Sometimes having them take notes and write related information down solidifies the learning.

Of course, some people use a combination of any of the above learning methods. For this very reason, I try to incorporate all styles in my workshops and learning sessions. Repeating information in different ways also helps solidify the learning.

Values and Behaviors

One of the most powerful learning experiences comes through an examination of one's own self. The way we act toward others is based upon our attitudes, which are shaped by our values. Our values are at the core of what makes each of us who we are. Simply put, they are what we treasure most. Most of us share values such as honesty and being treated with respect, but how we define each of those terms may differ from person to person.

Whether or not we are consciously aware of what our values are, we always act upon them or choose not to act upon them. If we are acted upon—our values affect our attitude. Essentially, an attitude is a way of acting and feeling that shows our disposition.

There is a finite amount of time between the time we have a feeling or give an action about something that we see or hear. Those who learn to evaluate how they will act, and not just react

DIVERSITY AT WORK   151

to stimuli, are much better off in the long-run than those who do not.

Our behaviors are closely related to our attitudes, which are closely related to our values. Effective leaders and diversity thinkers are masters at evaluating situations. They do not act not on impulse; but on an understanding of how their values and attitudes may come into play.

Humans are gifted with the ability to make choices on how we are going to act and react in every situation. However, not everyone recognizes that ability and sometimes they find themselves in less than desirable situations because of it. Every person seeking to be most-effective should cognitively realize that we always have a choice. Sometimes that choice is whether we are going to choose to be happy or not in each situation.

Assessing Biases and Prejudices

One powerful tool that I like to use in my diversity workshops helps participants see for themselves what their prejudices and biases are. The tool works very simply. It involves asking participants to be absolutely honest with themselves. Participants are promised that their answers to the following assessment will be kept confidential. They will see their own answers. The assessment tool consists of a blank piece of paper, a writing utensil, and a list that I usually put on an overhead (PowerPoint) display. I challenge you to take the assessment yourself.

Taking the test is easy. Simply put your first thoughts associated with each word on the list. Do not question what comes to your mind when you come to each word from the list. Just put it down. On your sheets of paper first put the word from the list then after that word, quickly write down as many thoughts that you associate with that word. Do not evaluate your first thought list until you are finished with the complete list I share with you.

- Women
- Men
- African-Americans
- Caucasians
- New Yorkers
- Gays
- Hispanics
- Disabled
- Californians
- Asians
- Teachers
- Latinos

Now after you have completed your first thoughts list, think to yourself what the list may be telling you about how you feel about certain groups of people. Which ones had the most negative words next to them? Which ones where most positive? Why do you think you feel the way that you do about each one? Just be aware of it. Know what your biases and prejudices are. Our honest answer comes quickly to our minds; when we question ourselves and second-guess ourselves, we run into the most trouble.

Remember, you are more effective in your life when you are aware of your biases and act on them appropriately and proactively. Life is much more fulfilling when we create powerfully-positive relationships with every person we meet. How many other group/classifications can you think of to try this assessment with?

I ran a workshop once when a man had very strong feelings against African-Americans. He could not even think of anything positive about them. He was not embarrassed about how he felt about it and believed he was justified for feeling that way. I told him that I would not judge him, but respect his feelings and appreciated his openness in sharing how he felt.

In that same workshop, I later shared a story about a New Yorker, a Caucasian man walking down a dark alley at night. An African-American male saw the White male and called out and started running toward him. The white male quickly started to run away from the African-American male, until he got into his car and sped off.

The African-American male was visiting from Seattle and was lost on the streets of New York. He had misplaced his wallet and desperately needed help.

How would you have reacted to this situation? What if the person who was lost was Caucasian? Would you have acted differently? Why or why not?

Diversity Terminology

Every good training session should help learners get on the same page and understand some basic terms. Terms that should be discussed in diversity training should include: Diversity, affirmative action, prejudice, discrimination, racism, sexism, assumptions, biases, values, flexibility, glass ceiling, and stereotypes.

I challenge you, as I do with my workshop attendees to write your own definition to each of those words. Then take out a dictionary and see how you did.

Skills for Managing Diversity

In summary, diversity training should do a variety of things. It must help people build diverse people skills. It must help members become aware of how culture impacts the organization. Members must also learn about their own cultures and how they affect their own personal values and behaviors. Likewise, diversity training should help individuals recognize their own biases through reflection of past experiences. Interaction skills come as a result of active education.

Diversity thinkers challenge their own assumptions, biases, and prejudices. They understand and value diversity. They see people as individuals who can actively play a part in benefiting their own organizations. They also act and speak in ways that are respectfully sensitive and appropriate to each individual. Effective leaders understand that every person is different and the key to having successful relationships with others is to treat them how they wish to be treated, not the opposite. They always act with integrity and honesty.

Effective leaders who practice diversity thinking know that there are many ways to accomplish goals. They therefore, encourage others to share their ideas and points of view. They get to know every person they meet as individuals, rather than stereotype them.

Effective leaders are flexible and look for the individual strengths of their followers and recognize their potentials. They take the time to genuinely tell each subordinate at least once a week why they appreciate them and praise them for something specifically well done.

Effective leaders who are diversity thinkers are active and not reactive people. They know that they have the conscious choice regarding how they will react in every situation. It is these leaders who have the ability to take their organizations to the next level and beyond the abilities of their competition that does not.

Effective leaders know that communication is both an art and a science. They realize that every person learns differently, and they must adjust their communication style to meet the needs of those they speak with. They speak clearly and concisely, using words that will be understood by the intended recipient. They are respectful in the ways in which they speak to others and are always considerate of others' preferences and needs.

Chapter Ten Review

I encourage you to answer the following questions. What are the four major steps of diversity training? How might they be used in your personal and professional setting? What are the most common conclusions drawn from diversity ice breakers? What other ideas do you have for an ice breaker in a diversity seminar? What different learning styles exist in your company? How can you tell what other people's learning styles are? What type are you? How is effective communication accomplished in your environment? What personal characteristics must be examined in order for diversity training to be most effective? What leadership qualities do you have? What leadership qualities do you feel you need to improve?

CHAPTER ELEVEN

BE THE EFFECTIVE LEADER

The following is an essay on how I view an effective leader and diversity thinker. Take some time and evaluate if you agree with my statements. What would you add to it? What would you change? How many areas sound like leaders you know? How much of it describes who you are? What would you change about yourself?

Effective Leaders

Leaders are not leaders if they do not have followers. Managers are not as effective as they can be if they are not leaders. Effective leaders know what they know and know what they want to learn about. They surround themselves with a diverse faction of people who can bring new ideas and talents to the group.

Effective Leaders know how they are and understand why they believe what they do. They are aware of their biases and prejudices. They are master-communicators. They are sympathetic to the needs of others. They know where they have been and where they wish to go. They are visionaries and help others to understand their own vision and how each individual has a specific role in helping bring that vision to fruition.

Effective leaders are flexible and masters at listening. They do this by concentrating on the words they hear and paraphrase back what they believe they heard. They show respect to every individual they meet. They do their best to create positive relationships with their coworkers and recognize every individual's talents and strengths.

Effective leaders are diversity thinkers. They see the value in every person of the organization. They openly show respect to those individuals using the requisites expressed by those individuals. They openly welcome input and ideas from followers and create working environments where people are motivated to give their best, because they never shut anyone down.

Effective leaders know who their customers are and build workplaces that reflect the diversity of their clientele. Effective leaders are proactively incorporating diversity thinking into all areas of their jobs. They know that utilizing diversity thinking in all areas equates to more creativity, greater production, profits, and an overall stronger organizations. Effective leaders are diversity thinkers, the only leaders of tomorrow.

Challenge to Grow

I thank you for taking the time to read and reflect on words in this book. There are many books on diversity available. I recommend that you not stop here, but continue on your journey for personal growth. Do research to find publications that enhance your life.

Take time each day to read something that increases your level of understanding. I challenge you to get to know who you are better. Challenge your beliefs, biases, and prejudices as much as you can. Be OK with who you are and change the areas in your life which you are not proud of.

Make promises to yourself that you actually keep. When you can promise yourself something and follow through on it, you will know the strength of your own integrity. You can take pride in yourself and know that you always do the right thing for the right reasons.

When you act with such commitment, others will also know you as a person of integrity. Others will treat you as you wish to be treated, because you know that you are truly worthy of being respected.

Leaders are powerless without the respect of others. Respect is earned and requires a continual process of maintenance and integrity. Diversity thinking is aligned with that very principle.

Think about how you wish people to think of you after you are gone. What will they say? Will they speak highly of you? Will they know who you were? Will they truly know you for who you thought you were? If we can live our lives like we are on a mission to respect others and gain the respect of others, we can be confident that our actions and lives were not in vain. Author Stephen R. Covey discusses these principles in his books more.

Be proactive in creating a life that you are proud of. Stop doing what you are not proud of. Take control of areas of your life that need to be controlled. Don't worry about areas of your life that you cannot control. Learn from your mistakes and actively evaluate how you could avoid similar mistakes in the future. Learn as many lessons as you can and share them with others freely and openly.

Hereafter is my own leadership diversity statement. After you read it, I suggest you create your own. Assess how you feel about each of the statements. Create an active opportunity to get to know yourself on a deeper level and welcome the personal growth. This type of growth will come through such an assessment and writing exercise.

PERSONAL DIVERSITY STATEMENT

I believe in hiring people of diverse cultural backgrounds to support the demographics of the areas they serve. By doing so, people of similar backgrounds will feel more comfortable about interacting with the organization. It also helps promote new ideas that people can relate to and benefit from. When people of diversity groups are hired and promoted to positions of responsibility, it helps illustrate that working hard yields rewards for everyone—not just a single elite group.

Personally, I surround myself with friends of diverse ethnicity and beliefs. My life is powerfully-enriched because of it! I have been successful in working with people of numerous cultural backgrounds because I know who I am and show others that I genuinely appreciate who they are—with little pre-judgment and with an open mind. Diversity thinking and being culturally aware is tantamount to success. I am genuinely dedicated to doing my part in helping every person I come in contact with to be successful and content on a daily basis. Because I value diversity.

Sincere wishes of success,
Paul L. Gerhardt, Ph.D.

DIVERSITY QUIZ

How confident are you in what you know about other cultures? On the next page, there are a few questions from a diversity quiz that I share with my workshop participants. You may be surprised at what you know and do not know. If you are interested in finding the answers to the quiz talk to others around you who may know the answers.

You of course can contact me for more information regarding leadership and diversity. I welcome your questions and comments. Take the diversity quiz on the following page.

1. What is "Parrandas"?
2. What is "Curanderismo"?
3. What is a longhouse?
4. What is a potlatch?
5. What month is Black History Month?
6. What is the Black National Anthem?
7. What does the Hawaiian term "Pau Hana" mean?
8. What does the Korean word "Chu-Sok" mean?
9. What month is mental health celebrated in?
10. What is generally eaten in the southern states on New Year's Day?

REFERENCES AND
SUGGESTED READING

- Beitler, M. A., (2006). *Strategic Organizational Change*. Greensboro, NC: PPI.
- Beitler, M. A., (2005). *Strategic Organizational Learning*. Greensboro, NC: PPI.
- Benavides, F.G., Benach, J., Diez-Roux, A.V., & Roman, C. (2000). How do types of employment relate to health indicators? Findings from the Second European Survey on working conditions. *Journal of Epidemiology & Community Health*, 54, 494-501.
- Carr-Ruffino, N. (2005). *Managing Diversity: People Skills for a Multicultural Workplace*. Boston, MA: Pearson Education Company.

- Covey, S. R., (2004). *Seven Habits of Highly Successful People*. New York, Free Press.
- Grossman, R. (March, 2000). Race in the workplace. *HR Magazine*, pp. 41-45.
- Hackman, J.R., Wageman, R., Ruddy, T.M., & Ray, C.L. (2000).
- *Industrial and organizational psychology*: Linking theory and practice (pp. 109-129). Malden, MA: Blackwell.
- James, J. (1996). *Thinking in the Future Tense*. New York: Simon and Schuster.
- Joplin, J. R.W., Daus, C. S. (1997). Challenges of leading a diverse workforce. *Academy of Management Executive*, August, 11, 3, pp. 32: 48.
- Judge, T.A., & Church, A.H. (2000). *Job satisfaction: Research and practice*. In C. A. Cooper & E. A. Locke, *Industrial and organizational psychology*: Linking theory to practice (pp. 166-198). Malden, MA: Blackwell.
- Leonard, B. (July, 2002). Ways To Tell if a **Diversity** Program Is Measuring Up. *HR Magazine*, 47:7, p21.

- Mathews, A. (Summer, 1998). Diversity: A principle of human resource management. *Public Personnel Management*, 27:2, p.175.
- Senge, P. M., (1990). *The Fifth Discipline*. New York: Doubleday.

Paul L. Gerhardt, PhD.
LeadershipSuccess Education and Support, Inc.
www.paulgerhardt.com
Dr.Paul@PaulGerhardt.com